Majalis al-ilm:

Sessions of Knowledge

RECLAIMING AND REPRESENTING THE LIVES OF MUSLIM WOMEN

Salima Bhimani

We acknowledge the support of the Canada Council for the Arts, the Ontario Arts Council, and the Government of Ontario through the Ontario Media Development Corporation Book initiative.

The Canada Council | Le Conseil des Arts
for the Arts | du Canada

ONTARIO ARTS COUNCIL
CONSEIL DES ARTS DE L'ONTARIO

National Library of Canada Cataloguing in Publication

Bhimani, Salima
    Majalis al-ilm, sessions of knowledge : reclaiming and representing the lives of Muslim women/Salima Bhimani.

Based the participation of 9 women in a series of forums.
ISBN 1-894770-05-6 (bound).--ISBN 1-894770-06-4 (pbk.)

    1. Muslim women--Canada. 2. Muslims--Canada. I. Title.

HQ1170.B445 2003   305.48'6971071   C2003-902999-9

Printed in Canada by Coach House Printing

TSAR Publications
P. O. Box 6996, Station A
Toronto, Ontario M5W 1X7
Canada

www.tsarbooks.com

Bismillahir Rahmanir Rahim

In the name of Allah the most kind the most merciful

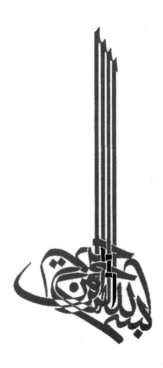

For the one whom I work in boundless love

Where do we start if not with our own self, diving into our inner cosmos.

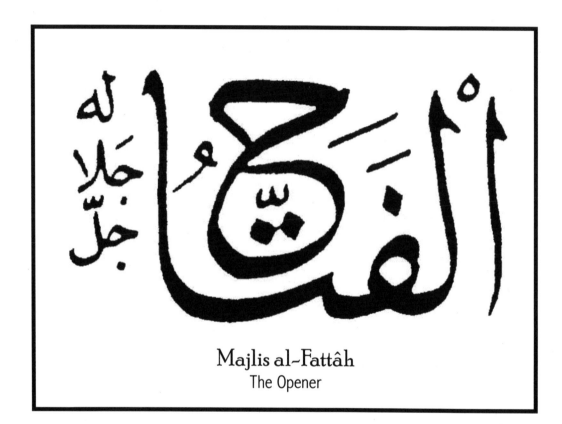

Majlis al-Fattâh
The Opener

July 1979. I was four years old. My parents, my brothers and I were coming home from prayers one night. The drive back was like an imaginary slumber party for me. I would fall asleep or have secret conversations with God about the day or have childhood fantasies and dreams. Somehow it seemed that we were all in different worlds. I could hear the others talking, but they seemed distant. As we approached our house that evening, I could hear the distant voices getting louder, coming closer. The next thing I knew we were in front of the house. Voices amplified. Present in the moment I looked up at our house. Toilet paper strewn all over it. Plastered with egg yolk. Spray-painted with words: "Paki Muslims."

"Having drunk entire seas, we remain quite surprised that our lips are just as dry as the shore and we continue to seek out the sea to dip them there, without seeing that our lips are the shore and we ourselves the sea."

Farid al-Din Attar (d. 1220)

As-Salaam alaykum (peace be upon you) and Ya Ali Madad. My name is Salima Bhimani and I would like to welcome you to Majâlis al-'Ilm (Sessions of Knowledge). Majâlis al-'Ilm is an opportunity for Muslim women to reclaim the power and right to tell the stories of their lives. We use these sessions as a forum to bring forth the narratives of our lives, a space to connect and challenge each other on issues that matter most to us. It brings together Muslim women's histories and experiences and their knowledge about the perceptions of them as Muslim women and the representation of Islam in society. These sessions are about resistance and challenge to reductionist, racist, sexist, and orientalist messages about Muslim women and Islam. This work is about community development and bridge building between Muslim and non-Muslim communities. It is also an educational and media tool for non-Muslim Western and Muslim audiences.

The nine women, including myself, that you will meet in this Kitâb al-'Ilm (Book of Knowledge) come from Sunni, Shia Ithnashari, Ahmadi and Shia Ismaili interpretations of Islam. Through this book we have critically explored what is known about "us" in Western society. We have created a production space in which to reconstruct our stories, which are complex, evolving, expansive and transforming, and our experiences as Canadian Muslims, and explore our relationships to Islam, the role Islam plays in our lives, our multiple and changing identities, our individual and communal struggles and what we know about one another, coming as we do from diverse cultural, ethnic and racial backgrounds. Thus, we are taking a hold of our own power to represent and speak for ourselves.

The Opener

As a child I recall having questions about myself as a South Asian Muslim woman. The various elements that helped shape my self-perception brought about a sense of shame and confusion about my ethno-racial and religious identity. I was confronted with stereotypes and prejudices about Islam as a violent, demonizing, oppressive, backward and ahistorical religion (in addition to the racism I faced as a young person of colour). Forced to face these encounters with non-Muslims who were stereotyping and discriminating against my religion, my people and my colour, I started thinking about what tools we needed as individuals and communities to reclaim ourselves and recreate stories about our lives and our histories. I became intellectually committed to addressing misunderstandings about Islam and Muslims within mainstream Western society.

I hoped also to challenge the ignorance among Muslim communities about the diversity within Islam. I thought about my Muslim sisters who came from little known tariqas (paths) in Islam and the frequent delegitimization of minority Muslim communities, which was just as troubling.

Various experiences of working internationally and locally on gender/women's issues, international development, and in community and cultural development awakened my mind and spirit to new ways of examining issues of race, class, gender, culture, faith and community development, which led me ultimately to this project. I realized that not only had I not heard stories from and about Muslim women in history, but also I was not currently hearing about Muslim women's experiences in the present. It was evident that neither the public school system nor religious institutions offered access to this information. When information was available it was negative, sexist and eurocentric. I attribute this to the fact that the information I was receiving came from biased Western and non-Western sources. If I heard from or about Muslim women from within the ummah (global Muslim community), it was information that was used merely to prove a version of Islam. Clearly, I was battling with ignorance from mainstream North American society, and a lack of knowledge about Muslim women within the ummah. I wanted to know if Muslim women themselves were talking about these issues and if so, where?

On television, in a magazine, or in an academic discourse it is more common than not to find messages and information about Muslims and Islam that are binary and unrepresentative. Images, stories, news reports, documentaries and ideologies have historically perpetuated Islam as violent and barbaric, Muslim men as militant chauvinists and Muslim women as oppressed, passive and sexually exotic. What is known about Muslim people and Islam is not limited, and in many cases it is ahistorical and without context and serves to reinforce stereotypes, Eurocentric versions of history, and the dominance and superiority of the West and Western civilization in opposition to Islam. I readily acknowledge that to reduce the West or the Western world as monolithic or representing one set of values is equally reductive and dangerous. Thus, when I refer to the West, I am speaking of the dominant values, judgments, structures and people that perpetuate or create relations of racisms, Islamophobia (fear or hatred of Muslims and Islam), and oppression, oftentimes, making invisible those people considered different from the dominant group. Western centrism has not allowed for other ways of knowing and other histories to inform the social, economic and political structures of society. Thus, if you do not fall into the dominant group, you are often left marginalized from full and fair participation, representation and consideration in society. This is the West to which I refer when speaking about the West and its relationship to Islam.

Most representations of Muslim women in popular culture are given in binary form and often in opposition to western women. ***Read: Muslim women = oppressed, Western women = liberated.***

Such dualistic readings of Muslim women's lives do not reflect the diversity of their backgrounds and experiences. Further, the polarization of Muslim and Western does not account for the diaspora of Muslim women born and residing in the West. Such a stark demarcation places Muslim women outside national identities. As Nehrei Tohidi (1998, 278), explains, "the notion of `Muslim women,' however, is more reductive because it diminishes the composite identity of millions of nationally, ethnically, economically and geographically diverse women to a single element, that is the religion of Islam. What usually underlies such an unidimensional identification is an essentialist perception of Islam, which sees Islam as a reified entity that has been the primary, if not the only factor in determining the conditions of women's lives." Thus, by showing how gender, culture, identity, media and other factors shape their lives, the participants in this project share their complex and diverse stories, and their thoughts and reflections as women who identify themselves as Muslim.

Certain discourses about the stereotypical Muslim woman oppressed by Islam end with liberation achieved through rejection of Islam. The story is often simplistic: Get rid of the religion, and the problem is solved. The practice of Islam in secular contexts is not what I find problematic. Rather, it concerns me that the wholesale rejection of Islam is due to its perception and manipulation as simply a political or patriarchal tool, without acknowledgment of it as a theoretical and pragmatic guide for relations between humans and their environment that can be humanistic and equitable. At the same time I do not support dogmatism and theological prescriptions. The relationship between God and the individual is a personal one. However, this project suggests that Islam as a way of life can offer much to women's daily experiences. The women in this book relate the complexities of belonging to various cultural and faith-based communities. They open up their lives and acknowledge the struggles within their communities and their faith, but they also celebrate the fact of being Muslim.

The focus of this project is not to create an alternative story to what is seen about Muslim women in the Western media, thereby merely reinforcing a dualistic view. Rather, we have shown that our lives, identities and knowledge are in constant evolution. Our notions of Islam and being Muslim are also being transformed with experience and knowledge. Most women in this group would not call themselves oppressed, but at the same time they would not deny the challenges that they and other women in their community face. They do not engage in a complete rejection of "Western values" but critically look at what is of benefit to them and what is not, at the same time creating what is their own unique experience in the West, a fusion of many influences that is constantly in transformation.

Let there be no compulsion in religion
(2:256)

Finally, Majâlis al-'Ilm is a revisiting and reclaiming of various aspects of Islam that I and the other women have found important-concepts, interpretations, and practices about which little is known in the mainstream. It is a way to break the one-dimensional perception and reading of Islam. We have attempted to share things about Islam that we are proud of and gain strength from. Thus, it is an opportunity for us to learn about Islam and its history, and those who practise, interpret and live the faith. This is a chance for non-Muslims and Muslims to get a deeper understanding of Islam and its followers. We also use this space to bring forth our personal politics, positions and analyses about issues that are taboo and those that have been intellectually hijacked by dominant views and perspectives, thereby rejecting the notion that Muslim women are passive or intellectually lacking.

About Muslim women.

To talk about the representation of Muslim women is perhaps misleading in that the statement in itself does not allude to the very historical configuration of Muslim women in the Western imagination. The perception of Muslim women is rooted in the historical past; in discourse about Islam and Islamic societies produced within the history of Western civilization, and the colonial and cultural hegemony of the West and its impact on Islamic cultures and Muslims. Although the aim of this book is not a historical examination of this representation, it is important to note that the representation of Muslim women today has developed over centuries and reflects the fact that Muslims and Muslim societies have not been the storytellers of their lives. Whether the narratives that we heard were from the Crusaders, Marco Polo, Orientalist historians or self-interested groups influencing the creation and passage of information in our societies, the Islamic character they portrayed was not multidimensional, which reinforced the otherness of Islam. The creation of this myth about Muslim women, and in effect the demonization of Islam, was and is both purposeful and dangerous. It has been a tool for political, economic and cultural dominance.

Today, worldwide, Muslim women constitute more than half of the one billion Muslims. Muslims can be found pretty much anywhere on the globe, though the largest concentrations are found in Indonesia and India. Set in a diversity of ethnic, cultural, racial and class backgrounds, Muslim women's lives vary in many aspects, including social, economic, political, cultural and religious. At present, most of the mainstream information about Muslim women does not come from Muslim women themselves, but rather from "outside" sources. Most often the conditions and realities of Muslim women's lives are reduced to Western centric and monolithic interpretations. These interpretations encapsulate their relations to their families, communities and state as simply patriarchal and violent, reducing them to mere slaves in these relationships. The women in this book challenge these notions and connect the multidimensional relations of culture, religion, community and individual.

"A distinct narrative representing the Muslim woman abides in Western cultures today. This narrative has formed a central part of Western discourse on Islam ever since the eighteenth century.

The expository tenets of the narrative are that Islam was innately and immutably oppressive to women, that the veil and segregation epitomized that oppression, and that these customs were the fundamental reasons for the general and comprehensive backwardness of Islamic societies."

(Kahfa: 1999)

About Majâlis al-'Ilm.

The concept of Majâlis al-'Ilm comes from the Islamic tradition of Majâlis al-Hikma which means "Sessions of Wisdom." The word majâlis means "sessions" (singular, majlis), and the word 'ilm means "knowledge." Hence, sessions of knowledge.

The Sessions of Wisdom were established during the Fatimid Caliphate (AD 909-1171). (The Fatimids named their caliphate after Fatima, the daughter of Prophet Muhammad (peace be upon him) and wife of Imam Ali, whom the Shia recognize as their first imam). During these sessions the religious teachers or the spiritual leader would pass on knowledge and converse with the seeker or pupil who wanted to learn more about Islam and its inner meaning.

Although I have based my own concept of Majâlis al-'Ilm on this tradition, I want to note that the Majâlis al-Hikma were special and private sessions between the teacher and seekers; in no way do I attempt to duplicate such a concept. What I take from this tradition and Islam in general is the notion that participatory knowledge creation, sharing and attainment are central to the expansion of humanity's relationship to itself and for the connection between the divine and the seeker. The notion that "knowledge is another facet of faith" is something that I have held very close in my own journey in life.

I want to point out also that during the Fatimid period scientific, philosophical and theological currents of thought flourished. The Fatimid leaders and community strongly encouraged dialogue among different groups, such as Jews, Christians and Muslims as an important way to cultivate intellectual thought. This history has significance for what we are to do in this book, reiterating the importance of the plurality that Islam has encouraged. Therefore, the cultivation and sharing of knowledge are central premises in confronting the issues raised in this project.

There are three basic assumptions underlying this project. One is that Islam and Muslims are pluralistic in interpretation and culture. The second is that the pursuit of knowledge for the expansion and betterment of our communities is critical for challenging oppression, racism and sexism. The third is that Islam can offer the means (language, theory and practice) that can be used to make these changes.

This project reveals the lives and stories of nine Muslim women, ranging in age from twenty to thirty-five and representing diverse educational and professional backgrounds. The one major prerequisite for this project was that each of the women identified herself as a religious Muslim. The definition of "religious" was left open to each woman's interpretation. It was important that these women identified themselves as Muslims, because I wanted to hear the voices of women who were using their interpretation of Islam as a part of their lives.

It is imperative to give voices to women from communities that have been historically, and are presently, marginalized and demonized (in spite of their great contributions to Islam throughout history). In this way we can start to destabilize and challenge dominant views within the ummah and make visible those histories that have become invalidated and make heard those voices that have been silenced. Women from the Shia Ithnashari, Shia Ismaili, Ahmadi, and Sunni tariqas have all contributed to this project. Secondly, it is important to give voice to women of different ethnic and racial backgrounds to challenge the geographical and cultural dominance of any one group, and to highlight the fact that Muslim women come from all over the world. Nazneen, Amber and Maha come from different parts of Pakistan, Farah comes from East Africa, and Zaynab from the Philippines. Munira is of Afghan and Swiss background, Mezghan is Afghan, Salwa is of Palestinian heritage and I am of Indian background. Most of these women also identify themselves as Canadians. Regrettably, I was unable to make the group as diverse as I had hoped for.

We met as a whole and in smaller groups to discuss a range of issues, from the role of Islam in our lives, to gender, identity, media representations of Muslim women, and community development. Most of what you will find in this book was gathered from these group and individual sessions. We have also included stories about our female role models. It is important to note that I have played different roles throughout the process of this project. I am the director of this project, the facilitator and participant in the group discussions and the creator and author of this book. I expose my multiple roles so that my own subjectivity and personal and political positions are woven into the book.

We hope that our discussions, stories and thoughts will provoke further dialogue among readers. We hope also that this book will prove useful for organizations, communities, educational institutions and the media as an educational tool. We do not attempt to come to any conclusions; rather we strive to reflect the dynamic ways in which we think and live, thus leaving questions, thoughts and reflection open for engagement.

Each woman you will encounter has different ways of living her Islam, but what is common is that each is committed to her intellectual and spiritual search. All of these women are committed to building communities that are equipped with knowledge and tools to build a humanistic Islam and life experience.

The women in this book have given me a sense of hope that we can work within and across difference. We pray that this book not only elicits ideological transformation but also inspires people to action for justice and equity and peace. This project is one among many that show that there is great hope for us as Muslims and marginalized communities to address issues collectively, and that there is growing commitment to do so.

One other aspect that needs highlighting is that grounding this project in Islamic concepts and language is vital to reclaiming our voices as Muslims. Often, Islamic words and ideas in the mainstream media are used to present a very scary Islam, embedding the "scariness" in religious terms, thus suggesting that violence and terror are religiously mandated and that those who follow the religion are therefore violent. Concepts such as jihad and fatwa are tainted. Secondly we hear Islamic terms and names only when they are used for terrorists or dictators, such as Saddam or Osama, or for missiles and bombs. This usage of terms and concepts, misrepresents Islam. We reclaim this space by reintroducing Islamic language and concepts to speak about Islam in positive and multidimensional terms. You will thus find Arabic used in many instances in this book because of its importance in Islamic history.

Before and beyond September 11

On September 11, 2001, for those of us living in North America and for those of us who had never experienced such large-scale violence and loss of life, our world was profoundly shaken. We are saddened that such an atrocity took place.

With that one incident, however, has come a growing snowball of violence, taking the form of hate crimes against Muslims, Arabs, and other minority groups, slander against Islam, and outright invasion and war in Afghanistan and Iraq. With the aftermath of September 11, came the increased polarization between Islam and Muslim countries and America in particular. Insidious in the "us" and "them" language was a frightening message to Muslims. Muslims living in North America were forced to choose which side they belonged to. Their nationality as Canadian Muslims was separated and brought into question.

In all the mainstream media coverage and the endless stream of books that have come after 9/11, one of the areas that has been least explored has been the impact of 9/11 on Muslims, as citizen of Canada and the US, who have been directly affected as the recipients of continued hostility and backlash and slander against Islam. When Muslims were heard from, they tended to speak in apologetic tones, having to somehow prove that those involved in the attacks were not "real" Muslims. This left very little room for Muslims to be involved in political and critical dialogue. Not only were Muslims invisible in the discourse after September 11, but also they were not recognized as having been directly affected by 9/11 as families, friends and fellow citizens of the victims.

So, what are the thoughts and experiences of Muslims regarding the event? Why do they think it happened? These are also some of the questions we have begun to explore in this book.

It is clear that September 11 set the stage for the escalation of negativity and misunderstanding about Islam, Muslims, Arabs and those associated in any way with Islam. This book however is not in response to 9/11. (This project officially began in Sept 2000.) We are responding to a history of Islamophobia (fear, hatred, and discrimination against Islam and Muslims), which can be traced back to the beginnings of Islam (610 AD). In general we place 9/11 within a global history of violence perpetrated by governments, corporations, armies, dictators, criminal justice systems, the media, and others, even though 9/11 may have had particular reasons and definitive targets. As a result, we do not set the values of the lives lost on 9/11 any higher than those lost elsewhere. We honour and recognize all lives lost in war, famine, and disease and through all types of human injustices throughout the world.

Final thoughts.

I have already stated that we were not able to reflect the diversity we had hoped for. I want to acknowledge that although Muslim women from other traditions in Islam, such as the Sufi tradition and other Shia traditions, are not present, their experiences and stories are nonetheless equally important and need to be heard. I also acknowledge the absence in this book of our other brothers and sisters who come from other marginalized communities, such as Muslims who are homosexual. These voices must be heard in order to further confront the alienation and silencing that many Muslim people experience.

The women in this group cannot and do not speak for their respective communities and interpretations of Islam. They are here as a microcosm of something larger. In some cases they may represent the general traditions or belief systems of their tariqa but they also reveal their personal, fluid relationships with their creator, their community and one another.

Allah is the Protector of those who have faith: from the depths of darkness He will lead them forth into light.

(2:257)

We are not fragments but the many facets of Spirit

Majlis al-Wâsi'
The All Embracing

In 610 AD the 40th year in the life of Prophet Muhammed, receives first revelation

Will receive revelations for next 23 years

Initially lots of resistance to message of Islam

Basic message:: Belief in One God.

Prophet Muhammad is the Seal of Prophets in the Line of Prophets (which include Jesus and Moses)

Initial message of Islam - one about social justice and equality. For women, slaves, orphans, those disenfranchised.

All revelations compiled in the Holy Book, Called "Qur'an

First Convert to Islam was Prophet's wife Bibi Khadija

Islam belongs to Abrahamic Tradition - which includes Judaism and Christianity

Islam means - Peace

Muslim is someone who submits to the will of God

Allah is the Arabic Term for God

Islam spread to many parts of the world. One of its glorious periods was in Spain - Islam present for 800 years

One of the goals of this project is to represent the various sects and interpretations of Islam. Rarely are the contrasting experiences of women from varying interpretations of Islam heard or talked about. Moreover, it is generally unknown that there are two major divisions in Islam that have differing tariqas and interpretations. Sunnis are the dominant group in Islam, both in numbers and representation, and are the ones whose voices are most often heard. Even historically, smaller groups such as the Ismailis, Ithnasharis and Ahmadis have been marginalized, their histories obscured and their cultures in many cases destroyed. This ignorance about the various interpretations of Islam is also a problem within the ummah. The information that we hear about each other is often antagonistic, negative and biased. I have been shocked on a number of occasions to hear my Sunni brothers or sisters state that they were told in their mosque that Ismailis are heretics. As a result, it is integral to this project to bring forth these varying interpretations and histories, to illuminate the diversity and plurality both in practice and in interpretation about which the people in the West have little knowledge. In addition, this gives us an opportunity as Muslims to learn about each other, without antagonism and fear. The interpretations of Islam should not be seen as a limitation or a fragmentation of the religion but rather as the dynamic ways in which it is experienced and lived.

Thus, revealing this "his-story" should serve to educate non-Muslims and Muslims alike. It is disheartening to read "historical" accounts, opinions and information written by Muslims who discount the stories, experiences and voices of Muslims different from them. The following is a very quick overview of the general differences and commonalities shared by the branches represented by the women in this project.

The diversity of Muslims and Islamic traditions.

The two major divisions in Islam can be attributed to the differing views about who would lead the community after the death of the Prophet. This was more than a political issue. For the Shia, it was also a question of spiritual guidance and authority. The Shia believed that leadership should remain within the family of the Prophet, known as the ahl al-bait. Ali, the Prophet's son-in-law and first cousin, was believed by the Shia to have been appointed by the Prophet. The Shia also believe that the Prophet entrusted Ali with spiritual knowledge.

The Sunnis, on the other hand, believe that the Prophet had not designated his successor. They believe that the followers of the Prophet chose Abu Bakr (father of Aisha, one of the Prophet's wives) as the political leader. This group came to be known as the ahl al-sunnah wa'l-jamâ'ah, the people of the tradition and consensus.

The Sunnis recognized a need to have a framework for interpreting the Qur'an. They did not, however, accept the Shia belief that Ali and his progeny would be the authorized interpreters of the Qur'an.

The Sunnis believed that there were only two things that were needed to practise Islam-the Qur'an and the Sunna of the Prophet. Following the Sunna of the Prophet meant modeling one's life on the life of the Prophet. Thus, the way that the Prophet handled situations would be the guide that would help interpret the Qur'an. The compilation of the Prophet's words and actions came together in volumes of books that were called Hadiths. The most famous hadith collection is the Sahih of al-Bukhari.

The Sunnis also developed two very important disciplines. The first, Tafsir, focused on the interpretation and explanation of the Qur'an. The second, Fiqh, laid the groundwork for rules of conduct and established principles by which new rules could be derived from the Qur'an and Hadith. Malik b. Anas (d. 796), Abu Hanifa (d. 767), al-Shafi'i (d. 820) and Ahmad b. Hanbal (d. 855), laid the groundwork in Fiqh teachings (for the Sunnis). The Sunnis continue to be led by the Ulama, who are scholars that provide guidance to them.

The Shia stress the importance of the esoteric dimension of the Islamic revelation, insisting on a balance between the exoteric and esoteric dimensions, between the law (Sharia) and its spiritual essence. Neither can exist without the other. They believe that there is an outer and inner meaning to all things: zahir and batin. This dual meaning, they argue, necessitates the existence of the Imam. The Imam does not alter the essence of the Qur'an but helps

I am the city of knowledge and Ali is its gate (saying of Prophet Muhammad)

foster an interpretation that can speak to the conditions of the community in its particular time. The Imam's role is to help the followers gain inner knowledge of the self and, as a result, of God.

The two major Shia tariqas are the Ithnasharis (Ithnâ 'Ashariyyah) and the Ismailis (Ismâ'îliyyah). The Ithnasharis are the largest Shia group. The split between the Ithnasharis and Ismailis occurred over the succession to the fifth Imam, Ja'far al-Sâdiq (d. 765). The Ithnasharis followed his youngest son, Mûsa al-Kâzim, and his successor Imams up to Imam Mahdi (end of the ninth century AD), who they believe is in occultation and will reappear to guide the community. Since then the Ithnasharis have been led by scholars who exercise guidance on behalf of the absent Imam.

The Ismailis, on the other hand, followed Jafar al-Sadiq's elder son, Ismail (the sixth Imam), thus their name, al-Ismâ'îliyyah. The Ismailis have followed this hereditary line of Imams until the present day; they are led today by the 49th Imam, the Aga Khan IV, who the Ismailis believe is the direct descendant of the Prophet Muhammad (pbuh) through Imam Ali and his daughter Bibi Fatima.

Imams Ali and Jafar al-Sadiq emphasized the central role of the intellect in searching for and discovering the layers of meaning in the Qur'an. The present living Imam of the Ismailis expresses this tradition in the following way:

"In Islamic belief, knowledge is two fold. There is that revealed through the Holy Prophet and that which man discovers by virtue of his own intellect. Nor do these two involve any contradiction, provided man remembers that his own mind is itself the creation of God. Without this humility, no balance is possible. With it, there are no barriers. Indeed, one strength of Islam has always lain in its belief that creation is not static but continuous, that through scientific and other endeavours, God has opened, and continues to open, new windows for us to see the marvels of His creation."

The All Embracing

As various disciplines within Islam were growing during the eighth through the tenth centuries, so was Sufism, which is a tradition that emphasizes a personal interpretation and close relationship with God. This relationship intensifies the life of the soul and the intellect. There are both Shia and Sunni Sufis. The Shia Sufis looked to the Shia Imams for guidance towards enlightenment. The Sunni Sufis were given guidance by the Murshids, who were spiritual masters who had attained spiritual enlightenment. The foundations of Sufism were laid by (the Shia Imam) Jafar al-Sadiq, Rabia al-Adwiya, al-Junayd, Mansur al-Hallaj, Abu Yazid al-Bistami, Dhu al-Nun al-Misri, among others.

The Ahmadis (Ahmadiyyah) are another tariqa represented in this book. There are many misconceptions about the Ahmadiyya movement, as there are of other smaller groups in Islam. The Ahmadiyyah movement was founded in 1889 in Punjab by Hazrat Mirza Ghulam Ahmad. He named the movement after Prophet Muhammad (who was also known as Ahmad) who embodied the qualities of "tenderness, gentleness, love and mercy." Mirza Ghulam appeared at a time when some Muslims believed that Islam was facing a crisis brought about by the attacks of Westerners and Christian missionaries. There was a general feeling that Islam was in need of a revival. Hazrat Mirza appeared as a proponent of the forgotten spirit of Islam. He received his inspiration from God and was believed to be the awaited messiah. The major principle that the Ahmadiyya movement claims is that Islam is a peaceful, loving religion and must be lived and propagated in that light. The movement was carried on after his death by various leaders, who developed the Ahmadiyya Anjuman Isha'at Islam (Ahmadiyya Association for the Propagation of Islam) founded in Lahore, Pakistan.

What the Shias, Sunnis and Ahmadis share is the belief in the concept of Tawhid (the oneness of God) and the Prophet Muhammad as the last and final prophet, the Seal of the Prophethood. This is an admittedly sketchy account of the beginnings of Islam and its two major divisions, Sunni and Shia. However, the objective of this brief glance was to highlight the distinctive approaches and rich history of the various Islamic traditions.

Oh Allah send your blessings on Muhammad and his Family

I will no longer be immured in a disparaging reality

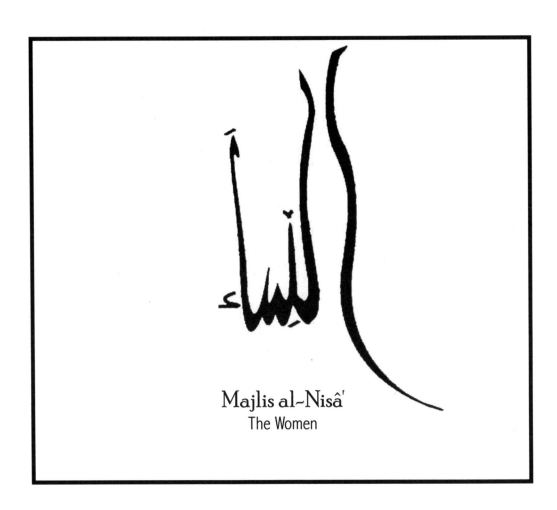

Majlis al-Nisâ'
The Women

Salima Bhimani

And if all the trees
On earth were pens
And the Ocean (were ink),
With seven Oceans behind it
To add to its (supply),
Yet would not the Words
Of God be exhausted
(In the writing): for God
Is Exalted in power,
Full of Wisdom.

(31:27)

Salima's Symbol

Beloved in your being I have perished into particles of love.

Since entering this existence, my stride and my words all dance to your rhythm; in sweet aching longing they strive to reflect you.

You often remind me of the many existences in which I have found you in breath, I have found you in light, I have found you in the roots of the earth, and in the creatures of life. Even when I have left you, you have never left me. Many times I have taken my focus away from you, reaching out to others, but you gently and patiently bring me back to your essence.

There is no other lover who is immersed in every molecule of my being. Exalt Love to its true status. GOD.

In this wisdom lies liberation.

Salwa Steitieh

Salwa's Symbol

Prayer Rug

Prayer is not just a ritual part of my obligations. It is truly an opportunity for me to get away from the world for the prescribed times of prayer and find an inner space that is reflective, cathartic and cleansing. When I go to prayer, I find a sense of peace and an immediate sanctuary as I stand on my prayer rug facing the qibla (holy site in Mecca for Muslims). It is a moral elevation and a purification of the body and soul. In a world where we are tempted and overwhelmed with so many desires and messages, prayer offers me an inner space to retreat from it all. Oddly enough, when I am not performing my prayers for reasons of exemption, I find myself at a loss and somewhat irregular in spirit. Once I resume my prayers, I feel stabilized again. It offers me balance in a world otherwise unbalanced so that I may establish worship to Allah (subhanahu wa-ta'ala [He is glorified and exalted]) and serve Him properly.

I was born and raised in Canada. My parents moved to Canada in the 1960s, when the doors to immigration were wide open. They settled here in the hopes of providing a better life for themselves and their new family, as part of the Palestinian diaspora.

I have three siblings: an older sister, Mona, a younger brother, Anees, and a younger sister, Yasmine. I was fourteen years of age when my parents had Yasmine; this was a joyous event that marked a new beginning for our family. My family always instilled the traditions and principles of Islam into our daily lives. We were sent to school on weekends to learn our deen (spiritual matters) and to learn Arabic, the Qur'an, and to memorize the suras.

When I was in my first year of university, my father passed away from a massive heart attack. It was a hard time for the entire family and we all vowed to make sure our family stayed together, especially since my sister was only six years old and my mother now had to look after her family alone. Losing my father was the worst event of my life. Having witnessed death so close, as he died in front of my mother and me, I was left with many questions as to why it happened, and therefore I turned to Islam more than before. I realized that my answers were to be found in the bonding forces of Islam. There is an ayat in the Qur'an in Sura Ya'sin that reflects this peace: "So glory to Him in whose hands is the dominion of all things and to Him will ye be all brought back." Through my pain, I realized that all things, including man, were created by Allah (swt), and inevitably, we will all return to Him alone, be accountable for everything in our lives.

Although it might seem peculiar, I have a solid presence of fear and love for Allah (swt) in my life. I fear God in the sense that I am reminded of the possible consequences and punishments for my actions, therefore I am cognizant of everything I say and do. With this fear in place, everything I say and do invokes the love of God. I love God for what He represents in this world and the hereafter and I love the Prophet and his teachings.

In the world we live in today, with the varied realities and pressures of life, my jihad, my "struggle" or my "effort," is to continuously discover and explore our rich practices, traditions and principles and strive to live our religion based on our convictions and our love for God, our compassion and our tolerance, and our sense of humanity, justice and morals.

The Women

Islam plays an integral part in my life; it is my way of life. The quote that I like to recall from the Qur'an that reflects my belief is, "Indeed in the remembrance of God the heart finds peace." In submission to my faith, I am constantly following this path, performing not only the ritual obligations that are called upon us, but remembering always to put into practice our moral obligations. I believe that one's faith is never completely achieved as some sort of task or assignment. We are constantly evolving to make an effort to increase, Inshallah, our ibaadah, aql (capacity to think) and imaan (faith).

Ambereen Karamat Nasrulla

Ambereen's Symbol

Qu'ran-e-Shariff

Qur'an-e-Shariff (Holy Book) that my dad bought me. In the first page is inscribed, "Satan is Fire-1969." To me the Qur'an is a symbol of serenity. It is always watching over me. There was a fire in my home and this Qur'an was one of the last things to survive the fire.

La ikraha fi din (there is no compulsion in religion).

I grew up in a family in which religion was always present, not as a see-you-once-a-week kind of friend, but as the kind of beloved friend who is always around and stays without needing to be asked. If I had to pick my household's favourite catch phrase, it would be "La ikraha fi deen," "There is no compulsion in religion" (2:256). I've never been forced to do anything when it came to religion. My father taught his children to examine everything with a healthy, critical eye. Whatever he would discuss, whether medicine, art, literature, or architecture, inevitably, remarkably, it all looped back to religion. He's a living, breathing, example of a Muslim. It's his essence as a human being. He lives by example, he is an example.

My name is Ambereen Nasrulla. Call me Amber (pronounced Umber). My parents are from Pakistan and moved around a great deal when they were younger with the result that my sister was born in Chicago, I was born in the UK, and my brother was born in Toronto.

Some of my immediate family belongs to the Ahmadiyya movement in Islam. It's an Islamic sect that was founded in 1889 by Mirza Ghulam Ahmad in Qadian, a small village in Punjab, India. He claimed to be the expected reformer, the promised messiah of the world community of religions and I was taught that his spirit was to rejuvenate Islamic moral and spiritual values at a time when Muslims were dropping away from religion. The movement he started, and the community in which I grew up, promotes the purest messages of Islam - peace, universal brotherhood, and submission to the will of God. Within a century, the Ahmadiyya movement reached more than 170 countries, with its followers taking leadership roles in social projects, educational institutions, health services, Islamic publications and the construction of mosques. What I'm leaving for last, though, is the fact that Ahmadis are bitterly persecuted - jailed, even murdered - in some countries.

The Women

Not all Muslims accept Mirza Ghulam Ahmad's contention that he is a renewer of the faith. Though Ghulam Ahmad never made the claim himself, many mainstream Muslims insist that he claimed to be a prophet, which is regarded by them as a direct insult to the Holy Prophet Muhammad (pbuh), the Seal of the Prophets. Muslims regard this as heresy. I respect the teachings of Ghulam Ahmad, and I adhere to them, but I don't see much difference between what I grew up learning and what "other" Muslims learn. I feel sad that "sect" has come to mean division. At the end of the day, all Muslims are the same. I know this particularly after returning from Mecca, where there were throngs of Muslims of different sects, skin colours, cultural backgrounds and socio-economic positions. The Kaaba, Allah's house, is the great equalizer. Whether you're a CEO or a car thief, you walk side by side, barefoot and humble before the creator. It doesn't get any simpler than that.

Mezhgan Hakimy

Mezhgan's Symbol

The Scale of Justice

This symbol represents my relationship to God. I think God is the only one who can be absolutely just. I like this symbol because to God everybody is equal. He is the source of justice. He is fair to every body.

My name is Mezhgan Hakimy. I come from a beautiful mountainous province in Afghanistan called Bamyan (where the Bamyan Buddha statue existed). I was born and raised in Kabul, the capital of Afghanistan. I have experienced conflict, violence, destruction, homelessness and hopelessness. I realize that Islam is not responsible for all this but, instead, foreign hands using ignorant and unwise people in the country who have forgotten the teachings of Islam and use the name of Islam to justify their actions.

Living in Afghanistan, I experienced bombings and explosions everywhere. Many days during the year the schools were off because of the bombings. The few days that we went to school, the fear and horror of rockets hitting us did not allow us to study in peace. Several times, because of civil war, my parents had to send me, for several months, to stay with my grandfather in Bamyan, which is located in the centre of Afghanistan. One of these times I was about ten years old. It was hard for me to live without my parents and family for months in a village where I barely knew anyone. Political changes in Afghanistan often interrupted my education. It was different from here, where such changes do not make much difference. In Afghanistan, when a person in power, such as, defense minister or any other important person changed, many lives were taken, and there were bombings.

The Mujahedeen fought against Dr Najibullah at the time of Russians and claimed a jihad against the Russian occupiers, then took over Taliban Afghanistan. Everyday the situation got worse. As a result, feeling that our lives were in danger, we fled Afghanistan, leaving behind our relatives, and took refuge in Pakistan, where we were not welcomed. The severe living conditions due to unfamiliarity with the language and culture, lack of employment for refugees, and living in an environment which was very different from ours, created many problems and challenges for us.

The Women

Despite all these problems, I always wanted to study, no matter what problems we had to deal with. Unable to afford the local school, we enrolled in a school established by my uncle, my brother, and some other active members of the community. The school was run by a few individuals who had no teaching qualifications or experience. They worked day and night, selflessly devoted themselves to helping the children learn something. After I matriculated (completed the equivalent of grade 10 in Canada), I had a deep desire to go to college and pursue further education. But this was not possible. I had to work to support myself and my family. I started teaching in the same school where I had studied. I taught math and science up to grade 6. It was a wonderful but very challenging experience for me. I learned a great deal about children, responsibility, and commitment, and discovered my abilities and talents and the courage to struggle and succeed. The experience helped me to mature quickly: to think about the world, the society I lived in, and how I could contribute to reducing the problems of my people.

God was always with me, no matter what state I was in. I felt His presence helping me and guiding me through sad and difficult times. My strong faith in God's existence has played an important role in helping me deal with the many challenges I have faced. It has given me hope to live, courage to fight against despair, patience to endure hardships and smile even when I was unhappy. My faith has given me the courage to share the story of my life, which is something very personal and valuable to me. I am not doing this to send the world the message that a Muslim woman is strong, faithful and courageous, she is never oppressed. She will face and fight against any injustice that is brought upon her.

My goal in life is to become a lawyer so that I can fight not only for my own rights but also for those who are suffering injustice. The injustice and inequality that I have experienced in my life and witnessed have created this desire.

Monira Kayhan

Monira's Symbol

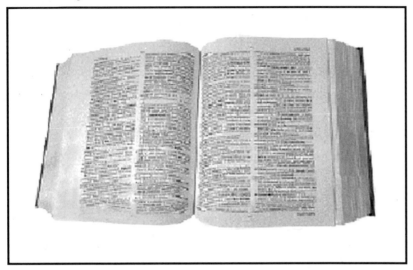

Book called, *My Sisters*

What is really nice about this book is that it was compiled by a Muslim sister who had gone through her own struggles to reach Islam. It is a collection of stories by the women she met through her journey. Every piece is amazing. I thought of the first time I talked to Salima (Bhimani) on the phone about this project and she told me that there would be women from different backgrounds, and different Islamic interpretations participating. As a part of this group I too wanted to help portray a unified image of Islam. In speaking to her I was reminded of this book and the author's journey in meeting these diverse women. I often pick up *My Sisters* and read a story from it and it inspires and encourages me.

I was born in Canada to parents who each emigrated from different countries. My father is a Muslim from Afghanistan and my mother is a Christian from Switzerland. My upbringing was fairly neutral in terms of religion. Both my parents are religious in name more than in practice, so as a child I was free to decide which faith I wanted to follow.

It was during my adolescent years that I felt a need to find my creator, God, and to further understand the purpose of life. Focusing mainly on Christianity and Islam, I searched for a religion that could answer my questions regarding topics I knew a little about, such as human behaviour, biology, ecology, astronomy and the like. I needed a religion that completed my thoughts and would help me grow into a better being. Islam was where I found my answers. The chaos of life was pieced together perfectly through the chapters of the Holy Qur'an.

At the time of my research, I had already been labeled as a very outgoing, independent, strong-minded woman. As a distant observer of Islam there were some obvious stereotypes that I had to investigate, many of them focusing on the role of women in society. At the very beginning of my research I was impressed with how many strong, educated and opinionated Muslim women I met, a far cry from the usual oppressed, uneducated and blatantly submissive Muslim women portrayed in the media. It was these women who helped me understand my role in society and the Islamic laws that concerned women.

As my research answered my questions and satisfied my concerns, I developed into the Muslim woman I am today. My journey, thus far, has been pleasant and without too many hurdles or disappointing encounters. My mother was my biggest supporter, especially when I started to wear hijab (head scarf). Every day I grow stronger in my faith, thanks to the help of God.

Islam is certainly my way of life. Everything I do involves Islam, it is my code of ethics and conduct, and it is my guide.

Farah Murji

Farah's Symbol

Tasbhi

Tasbhi (prayer beads representing the ninety-nine names of Allah) is one symbol for me because of the convenience. It is something physical that I can carry with me at all times. I have used a tasbhi for as long as I can remember and it automatically takes me to prayer and to God. Just reaching in my pocket or purse and feeling the beads is a physical reminder that I should not forget to balance my spiritual and material lives. It puts me in touch with myself and the greater purpose.

I am a Shia Ismaili Muslim woman. I was born in Toronto and proudly call myself Canadian. My parents were both born in Tanzania as was my paternal grandmother. The rest of my grandparents were born in India and then immigrated to Tanzania. I have not been to any of these countries, though it is one of my dreams to visit East Africa one day. I want to visit India, but my desire to see Tanzania is greater.

The Women

Being an Ismaili Muslim woman has impacted every aspect of my life. My parents have always encouraged and supported my education. I have been raised to be a strong woman, and it has been impressed upon me that independent and critical thinking are necessary, especially when it comes to religion. I think that this in particular has made me comfortable in my beliefs.

One of my fundamental personal beliefs is the equality of both genders. If my faith did not treat me as an equal member of society and did not instill in me the value and belief that I am as capable as men, it would not be a faith in which I would be able to be my true self. Equality of men and women is also displayed within our Ismaili institutions and our various councils. I have come to recognize and realize the relationship between culture and faith. Often, the inequality between the two sexes is blamed or, perhaps worse, justified by religion, when many of these schools of thought and practices can be explained in a cultural context. If a religion were innately sexist, this would be problematic. This is not to say that every issue can be simplified into a cultural issue. There are daily challenges that I face that require reflection, research and turning to those, such as my father, whose wisdom and opinions I value. Through these methods, if I'm lucky, I can establish a comfort level with the challenges that I face. It is with this understanding and the desire to seek knowledge that I can proudly say that I am not in a patriarchal religion, that I am not oppressed as a woman by Islam, and that I am free to be the independent, compassionate, motivated, opinionated, nurturing and strong woman I am today.

End note:

The Ismaili communities have many national and international institutions and agencies under the umbrella of the Aga Khan Development Network. Under this umbrella, there are institutions in place that address the diverse needs of the Ismaili community worldwide. The broad range of programs include primary health care in "developing" countries. and educational institutions, such as the Aga Khan University and Hospital, the Aga Khan Trust for Culture, which promotes Islamic culture through architecture and art, and many other arms of the AKDN with programs and services for the local and global needs and progress of the Ismaili community. These programs and services speak to both the material and religious aspects of the communities. On a local level, here in Canada, we have programs and projects that deal with various social issues (poverty, needs of the elderly, women's issues, etc.), settlement issues and youth programs. Ismailis are scattered throughout the world. The largest concentrations of Ismailis are found in China, Central Asia, and South Asia. If you would like to know more about the AKDN, please visit the following website: http://www.akdn.org.

Nazneen Khan

Nazneen's Symbol

The holy book Qur'an.

The holy book is the only thing that I connect to regarding my religion. The Qur'an provides me tremendous guidance and understanding. The teaching that most stands out for me is one that explains that if we want to get to know God, then all we have to do is look around us. Look at nature and we will find Him there. The Qur'an also tells us that God has given us aqal (ability to reason) and so it is very important that we use it to understand the Qur'an and its teachings rather than accepting things through blind faith.

Another section from the Qur'an that stands out for me discusses Huquq Allah, our obligation to God and Huquq ibad, our obligation towards humankind. Qur'an places greater importance on Huquq ibad, duties towards humankind. I share this belief that we are obligated to one another. The fact that the Qur'an states this so clearly reiterates to me that God has made us responsible to each other. To be responsible in our thoughts and actions is to be responsible to God.

The Women

I follow the Sunni tariqa, though I describe myself simply as Muslim. I was born in Rawalpindi, Pakistan but grew up in Jhelum in Pakistan. I have four brothers. My parents' names are Nasim Akhtar and Yaqub Khan. I came to Canada from Pakistan in 1992, in the midst of doing my Bachelor's degree. When I arrived, I had to complete grade 12 and my OACs. I then went to college for business administration and finance, where I learned about how to make money and how to be ruthless. I was pretty shocked that this is what we were being taught.

Since I was a little girl, I have loved to sing, to meet and see different people, and to visit peaceful places.

I have learned many things, especially from those closest to me. I have always been an observer. My mother and father have been great role models in terms of instilling values. But they not only talked about values that one should live by but also practiced them. My father always used to say, " I say what I do." I watched my parents live their goodness. Some people go to masjid (mosque) and pray but then they talk badly about other people or don't do things that are good. What is the point of praying? I am glad I had people to teach me to practise the values that I believe.

There was always a need for me to belong to God, but on my terms. Your relationship with your creator is a personal one. There is only you and God. No mother, no father, no brother and no sister.

The Qur'an talks about a complete way of life, giving insight into human nature. God has given us the fundamentals, such as the ability to think. The responsibility of every human being is to use these fundamentals for good. And that is a choice that God has given us, to use His gifts for the benefit of humanity and not for its detriment.

As Muslim women, our roles have a lot of impact. That is why it is important for me to be blunt about who I am and what I believe, to live everyday being thankful to God, as well as to impart to others the knowledge that I have gained and been given, and likewise to learn from them.

Maha Hussein

Maha's Symbol

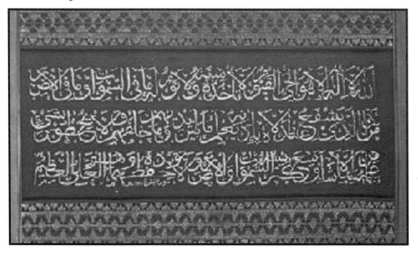

Ayatulkursi bracelet

A series of three verses from sura Baqara in the Qur'an.

Throughout the Muslim world you will find that people recite these verses to ward off evil and to keep themselves safe. It is very common for people to wear amulets, lockets or bracelets inscribed with these verses. I wear a bracelet like that because of an ayat: "Those who hold on to God, hold on to the firm handle that won't break." I find that extremely comforting. When I am going through a difficult period or feel truly in despair, that line comes to mind. I got the bracelet when I was fifteen or sixteen. When I initially got it, I would take it off every night and put it on my bedside table and then put it on every morning. Then one day I was supposed to meet a friend at the mall and I couldn't find it. I remember my mother thought I was crazy because I was looking for it so frantically. It was getting late, so I decided to leave. That day I was in a really terrible car accident. Had someone been sitting in the back seat of the car, I don't think they would have survived. Since then I have not taken the bracelet off. I am now twenty-five. I will never take it off.

I was born in Karachi, Pakistan. My father was a captain in the Pakistani merchant navy, so we sailed as a family for several years before settling first in the United States and then, ultimately, in Canada. I've lived in Toronto ever since I was twelve, although when I graduated from high school, I returned to the United States for university. I currently hold a bachelor of arts in anthropology from Princeton University, a course of study which proved instrumental in shaping my fascination with Islamic law, and particularly my belief that a humanistic interpretation of the sharia, one that espouses full equality for both sexes, and that is free of biases regarding gender, sexual orientation, race, class, and so on, is not only possible, but religiously permissible, and indeed, religiously mandated.

It was during my undergraduate years that I was first meaningfully exposed to the idea of exegetical inquiry as a fundamental right of all Muslims, a notion that I had considered superficially during high school, but which now exploded into my intellectual life like a grenade (smile). My decision to apply to law school, made just a few months ago, was largely fuelled by my commitment to that particularly intellectual project.

My history as a Muslim woman is inextricable from my history as a South Asian woman living in the global North. As a child, and then as an adolescent, my principal experience of Islam was as a set of cultural taboos and prescriptions that were presented as religious ones. My parents' views on things like dating, for example, had far more to do with their cultural identity as South Asians than with their religious beliefs, but they articulated their perceptions in religious terms rather than cultural ones. I don't think that the decision to couch their views in that particular way was a conscious one, but it was hardly an uncommon practice amongst first-generation immigrant families.

My own realization of my identity as a Muslim, and the realization that most of what was transmitted to me and most other Muslims as Islam was profoundly skewed, was for the most part a gradual process. The angrier and more depressed and disillusioned I became, the more I read, and the more I realized that what passed for Islam as most people understood it was a travesty, an absolute perversion of the faith as it was initially revealed and practised and, in my opinion, envisioned by the Prophet and many of the first Muslims at Mecca and Medina.

The Women

Realization was definitely a cyclical thing for me, in the sense that I would read and research because I was angry; then I would get even angrier as I read authors like Fatima Mernissi, Riffat Hassan, Amina Wadud Mohsin, Abdullahi An-Na'im, Farid Esack and others, because they made me realize that so much of what I had been taught was garbage, and had we only known it, my friends and I could have been spared many many bitter experiences at the hands of our parents, our mosques, our elders, our community, or whoever it was that was attempting to constrain our ability to think and act independently; then I'd get extremely depressed; then, invariably, some incident would occur involving me or a friend or an acquaintance that would make me so furious that I'd start reading again.

Zaynab

Zaynab's Symbol

It's a book called, *Islam the choice of thinking Women*

This book examines religions and cultures and describes historical patterns about the way in which women have been treated. It outlines the rights that the Qur'an has given to women in Islam. This helped me to make up my mind to turn towards Islam. It was a step forward. I have always been a feminist and very pro-women. (I shouldn't say that I am anti-men, but I guess sometimes I am.) I found that Catholicism didn't accord women sufficient rights (and the notion of the Trinity didn't sit well with me either). So in that sense, Islam gave me a perspective of women that I was looking for. It opened up a lot of doors for me. It brought me back to God. I was very spiritual to begin with, but my experience with Catholicism turned me off for a long time. This brought me back.

"In order to know her self in Islam, she needs to know her rights and duties towards God, her society and towards herself."

-Leila Bakhter

Oh, My God! Why? This is a common reaction I receive from friends and acquaintances when they learn that I declare myself a Muslimah (female Muslim). In many ways, I cannot blame them. After all, my previous lifestyle was somewhat colourful.

I am the first Filipina of my family to be born in North America. So, as you can imagine, I had a good childhood. My parents, like other immigrant families, did the best they could to give me everything. For that, I am eternally grateful. I was baptized a Roman Catholic. My parents and grandparents did not hesitate to instill in me a sense of the Almighty. The concept of God and the discipline of prayer were part of our household. I began to study catechism and the history of Catholicism, only to be disappointed. Every question I asked was not given a logical answer.

Throughout my high school and college years, there remained a void in my life. Then one year, I took a course in world religions and explored many different concepts. I immediately took an interest in Islam. Initially I fell victim to the ignorant and prejudicial view that Muslim women suffered from oppression. Strangely, my prejudices never prevailed and instead, my interests and thirst for knowledge increased.

Coming to Islam was the best thing I have done. But as in other aspects of life I find some aspects discouraging. I find that Muslims, like the Christians, are divided by culture and rarely do I see much unity. It is also discouraging to see men who use religion to support their own sexist and cultural views. What's worse is that some women are consciously ignorant of their religion of birth and of their rights.

Living Islam has become a part of my everyday life, as a woman and as a human being. I live every day to its fullest and do my best to be a good Muslimah. To be a good Muslim in my mind means being a better human being. It's easy to follow society's whims, but it's a challenge to stay on the straight path and apply your experience and knowledge to the betterment of society, your community, humanity and most of all, yourself. Inshallah, I hope to keep my strength. And unlike some, I love challenges.

The silenced invisible voices in Islam.

The intolerance and persecution of women and various Muslim groups within Islam is a serious problem that remains largely invisible and silenced. We dedicate this space to the stories of those women whose histories, visions, hopes and contributions have been erased, their experiences of Islam destroyed by oppressive structures and by those who supposedly preach Islam. These stories tell of the persecution faced by marginalized Muslim communities. These stories are about those women whose right to seek knowledge and find their God has been taken away through the distortion of Islamic law and patriarchal cultural practices. Most importantly these stories are about the defacing of people and their communities and, as a result, the fragmentation of Muslims. This is the story of one woman and her struggles against persecution.

Iran is a mountainous region, with the Caspian Sea touching its peripheries. It is a beautiful country, what was once a beautiful country where I was raised. Life for me as a young girl should have been about playtime and laugher and talking with neighbours, but that was not my experience. It is painful for me to recall that my childhood and youth were not filled with many fond memories. My parents tried to provide us with a happy, loving environment, but the violence and alienation from outside always crept into our happiness. The air was often filled with fear and caution, as opposed to peace and contentment. Why was my life in Iran so hard? You see, I am what many of you might call a minority, an Ismaili Muslim, from Iran. My identity as an Ismaili was cause for persecution against me, my family and my community.

Ismailis have a long history in Iran, going back hundreds of years, and yet we were treated as foreigners. Growing up in Iran meant denying our identity as Shia Ismaili Muslims. It meant living in hiding most of the time, not exposing our "differences." If we were found out, name-calling usually followed, and then brutal, physical violence. Nobody wanted to know who I was, who we were. It was clear that minds were made up that we were not true Muslims. Ninety percent of Iran is Shia Ithnashari, and even though we are Shia as well, we are considered illegitimate Muslims, heretics. We are a silenced minority.

Going to school meant hiding the fact that we were Ismaili, at least if we wanted to be safe and have a chance at an education. It was bad enough that we had to deal with regular, everyday childhood squabbles. We had to contend with never ending scrutiny and harassment if we were found out.

Can you imagine what it is like to live in hiding, in fear? One place where we all hope to feel closest to God is in our houses of prayer. In our house of prayer (or jamat khana as we call it), the dialogue with God was always interrupted. People would come and throw rocks in the windows and we would pray for protection and help.

This persecution of Ismailis was religiously sanctioned. We would hear about khutbas (speeches) in mosques that would rile up our Muslim "brothers and sisters" against us. These cruel messages would pierce our hearts and give us little hope of living without fear. It was an impossible situation. Anything we did or said was used to prove we were un-Islamic. For example, during times of war, there was a strong sentiment among Ismailis that we would become involved. We did not believe in war. This was seen as proof that we are not true Muslims. And if we were forced to go to war, and our people came back alive, we were told this was evidence that we were not true Muslims because we did not die in the name of Islam.

Like hawks circling above, our oppressors watched us, looking for anything they could use against us.

The Islam that we were taught was one based on fear. Everything was based on fear. I was taught that if I didn't wear the hijab, I would go to hell where I would be hung by my hair. Though I no longer believe this, I did once. They wished to scare us into obedience. I could not be free even in my own backyard. I had to make sure I wore the hijab, in case someone saw me and spread word of my indecency. If I did something wrong my whole community would be discredited and persecuted.

The Women

To this day I am uncomfortable calling myself Muslim because from my experience it is not a label I am proud of. How can I call myself a Muslim, when I know that fellow Ismailis are suffering in many countries from persecution? Ismailis are denied rights, such as education and the right to openly practise their faith. How can I align myself with the people who cause this? I am not ready to call myself a Muslim. I know that it is not Islam but those who persecute in its name who must be held accountable, and I do hold them accountable. But until something changes for those who are persecuted I will not call myself a Muslim.

In her stories we see our lives.

Majlis al~Khabîr
The Aware

The Aware

There are two distinct and dominant discourses about Muslim women. The first centers around the Western perspective of Muslim women as oppressed, passive, silent and sexually intriguing (which comes from Orientalist observers and historians). The second is found within Muslim communities about who the Muslim woman should be, what she should look like, how she should participate within her community and what her version of Islam should be. For the most part, the current dominant Western discourse about Muslim women is monolithic.

On the other hand, the discourse within Muslim communities or states is varied and is determined by diverse cultural influences, economic and political relations, religious interpretations, and history. The experience of Muslim women spans the spectrum of having a voice and negotiating their place in society, to having very little input. Likewise, Muslim women's responses to these diverse experiences within their societies (which includes the West) ranges from "I may see problems within my community, but I am not oppressed" to "There are issues of oppression that need to be addressed, and I have been oppressed." Indeed such varied experiences and perspectives are not exclusive to Muslim women, but reflected by the experiences of women throughout the world. We hope that through an exploration of our experiences as Muslim women we will be able to come up with a more integrated interpretation of our realities, than those offered by a binary, disconnected view that sees us as either oppressed or liberated and obscures the complexities of our lives.

O ye who believe! Ye are forbidden to inherit women against their will. Nor should ye treat them with harshness, that ye may take away part of the dower ye have given them,-except where they have been guilty of open lewdness; on the contrary live with them on a footing of kindness and equity. If ye take a dislike to them it may be that ye dislike a thing, and Allah brings about through it a great deal of good.

(4:19)

"Can a woman be a leader of Muslims?" I asked my grocer, who, like most grocers in Morocco, is a true barometer of public opinion.

"I take refuge in Allah," he exclaimed, shocked, despite the friendly relations between us. Aghast at the idea, he almost dropped the half-dozen eggs I had come to buy.

"May God protect us from the catastrophes of the times! mumbled a customer who was buying olives."

Fatima Mernissi (1991, 32)

All six women deconstruct and talk about how their experience of Islam and their communities are influenced by their gender.

Munira

I don't spend a lot of time thinking about how my being a woman affects my religion or my community. I am, however, aware that by being a Muslim woman, a Shia Ithnashari, who wears the hijab, there are definitely some stigmas and common misconceptions about me and women like me. I find that we as Muslim women are questioned much more and are compared with other women in the West. Physical appearance makes a difference, especially when there are so many negative associations with the hijab. Within the Muslim community there are also assumptions about the role of women, but my experience has been that there is not one expectation by the whole community. Rather, the expectation varies depending on the person you are interacting with. Some may want women completely involved in all aspects of a project, others may prefer to exclude women completely.

Nazneen

As a young girl in Pakistan, I was a nathka (one who sings devotional songs) in school and college. As a result, most people assumed I was really pious. I think that helped me get away with a lot. I was also protected by my brothers. People would try to tell me to do things, but I always followed the example of my mother. So in Pakistan I didn't really have any concerns around religion. But since coming to Canada I have faced challenges. People have expectations about what a Muslim woman from Pakistan should be like. I was expected to be a five-time-prayer woman. I was expected to set an example for others because I am from Pakistan, and, to be a certain kind of religious Muslim woman. They obviously don't know me.

Amber

As I was growing up, everyone talked about Islam as a religion of equality. I see that in my family but not at the community level. The dichotomy is frustrating. I find that my maternal instincts kick in, and I become protective about my religion. I don't always want to defend my experience as a Muslim woman because people assume we are oppressed.

The Aware

Mezghan

I think there is inequality between men and women everywhere in the world regardless of religion. Even in the developed countries women are not given the same rights and opportunities as men.

And Islam compares well with other religions. For example, the Qu'ran and the Prophet (pbuh) both assert women's rights and that women should be honoured and respected, which implies that within religions that existed before Islam women did not have many rights and were not well respected.

Being an Ismaili Muslim woman, I think I am given as many rights as men. Ismailism encourages research and finding the right path for oneself. I have choices that are probably not available in other sects. Education is given a great deal of importance among Ismailis. I feel very happy and content being an Ismaili Muslim. I have not experienced any inequality between the genders in the community. However, being a Muslim woman, I experienced difficulties while in Afghanistan and Pakistan. I didn't even feel safe going to school alone. I was afraid of being harassed by men. But I do not think Islam is to be blamed for that. In fact, Islam insists that women should be honoured and respected.

Maha

When you belong to a marginalized group, you are forced to be more critical in your thinking. You think about the conditions of your oppression, what they are rooted in, how they came about, what other processes they are linked to. Being a woman strengthened my faith because it forced me to investigate Islam more than those Muslims who don't feel constrained by religious restrictions.

You craft an interpretation that you can be happy with and that you find extremely fulfilling. But no one else may understand it, so it can be isolating in that respect, particularly when others think that you are a heretic. While it's definitely been a difficult process, this investigation has led me to a completely alternative, humanistic interpretation that is really beautiful and wonderful. When you discover the true essence of your faith, which has been hidden from you for so long, it's like the scales have fallen from your eyes; nothing looks the same after that. It changes you in a fundamental way. Being a woman in Islam forces you to be a lot more knowledgeable than Muslim men about their faith.

Zaynab

Much of my experience of men has been very negative. From the time I was a child, the only man I trusted was my father, not my uncles, nor even other kids. Growing up in an all-white neighborhood in Montreal, I was called all sorts of names, from "chocolate monkey" to "Chinese nigger," mostly by boys.

I had a horrible experience in high school when I was assaulted by some neighbourhood guys. The assault was racially motivated. I didn't tell my parents about it because they were already so protective and I didn't want to lose the freedom I had.

Islam has helped me deal with much of this. The more I read about Islam the more liberated I feel. I also believe in modesty, and rather than seeing men as strong, I see them as weak. I think that women need to be stronger. We have to work and live with men, and the only way we can do this right now is by practising modesty. Inshallah (God willing), in the future it will be different.

Farah

I think I am really lucky to be a woman in Islam. I have chosen to learn more because I have had questions and issues that I wouldn't have had as a man. As a woman you see things around you every day that you don't necessarily agree with. So, you have to go and research. Or you have to do some soul-searching to come up with your own interpretations.

Salwa

Growing up in a typical Arab family with one male sibling left me frustrated and disillusioned, especially during my adolescent years. There were levels of inequality at home between my brother and I. He received special treatment, and it was evident that he was the favoured child; but I knew enough of Islam to realize the difference was cultural rather than religious. This bias is probably similar in other cultures. The male in the Arab society and Arab family is regarded as a true patriarch. Arab mothers and fathers dote on their sons. And sisters are taught to respect their brothers. My family was no different. Truthfully, I was annoyed and irritated by this, but like all of us, I searched within Islam for the knowledge to clarify things in my head and to challenge those within my culture.

The dominant discourse from about the eighteenth century to the present basically states, often in quite sophisticated ways, that the Muslim woman is innately oppressed; it produces Muslim women who affirm this statement by being either submissive nonentities or renegades rebellious against their own Islamic world and conforming to Western gender roles.

This oppression is often figured as sexual oppression, and the corresponding submission or rebellion figured as sexual submission or rebellion. It is produced mainly in ways that are pleasurable from a heterosexual male perspective that rationalizes and justifies Western interests in the material domination of the Islamic world.

Kahf Mohja (1991, 10)

The Aware

I am comforted and proud that there is no difference between men and women with respect to their spiritual relationship and accountability to Allah (swt). Men and women are regarded as equal when it comes to issues of duty, obligation, practice, virtue, spirituality and, most importantly, knowledge and intellect. However, I am acutely aware that we are not the same. We are equal but not identical.

Salima

Being a woman and being Muslim was always a point of contention in my experience and mind as a young woman, even though I come from what I would deem a very progressive tradition in Islam. Patriarchal structures were part of Muslim communities (In my experience) and Canadian society as a whole. Stories of my religion and history were told from the mouths of men. I was told that Muslim women are less then men, less in the eyes of God due to their inherent fallibility, which comes from their purported irrationalism and limited capacity to think. So how could my gender not have an impact on my experience of Islam? At the same time it was clear that patriarchal ideas did not stem from any concrete theological basis. To add to this, the religious and political role models were all men.

When the women spoke, they often spewed out the same patriarchal rhetoric claiming that within Islam Muslim women are highly respected and what looks like subordination really isn't. This distortion and manipulation I could not accept, and I made a commitment to challenge my marginalization. My relationship with God and my growing understanding of my faith could not admit such oppressive ideas. I refused to allow Muslim women to remain on the fringes of their faith. It has been a difficult but highly rewarding road of deconstruction and reconstruction.

Moments that have influenced our notion of self, as Muslim women. Realizations we have come to.

Nazneen

About four years ago, I made three friends at school. Two were Sikh and one was Hindu. I spent a lot of time with them, but they seemed reluctant to discuss religion with me. I thought they might have some kind of image in their heads about me as a Muslim. Once, one of the Sikh girls was celebrating a religious event at her house and she invited me. In one room they had all the religious symbols. They took us inside and showed us around and explained the meaning behind all the stuff in the room. This was the first time I had a chance to get to learn about the Sikh community. I was very happy that day. That moment is very precious to me. I felt honoured to be included in their ceremonies. I felt that a barrier had come down between us. I felt good to be a Muslim.

Salwa

My self-awareness as a Muslim was raised at university. There I searched for deeper meanings behind my position and status as a woman in Islam within an academic framework. I read books on the subject, including Leila Ahmed's Women and Gender in Islam. This book helped me explore the many discourses of gender and Islam throughout history. It helped me to examine critically my position as a woman within Islam and to achieve a comprehensive understanding and appreciation of our true religion.

Zaynab

I am more aware of everything around me. I've gone back to my roots. I have always been interested in human beings and in humanity. You know the saying that there is only "one race and that's the human race?" I believe that. For a long time after I was assaulted, I forgot everything. I lived a life of illusion, partying, men, alcohol. Some people call that a normal college life, but I don't think it's normal. I don't think it's normal to live an illusion. Islam just brought me back to modesty; not that I am covered from head to toe. But I am more aware of who I am, more tuned to God, and I am a much happier person. I am more at peace with myself.

What has influenced your notion of self as a woman?

The Aware

Amber

When I was around seven or eight, my father would walk through the house at 5:30 in the morning saying the azaan (call to prayer). Our eyes barely open, my older sister and I would stumble to the bathroom to wash our faces and do ablutions so that we could pray with our dad. Now I'm lucky if I pray five times a week let alone the prescribed five times a day. But I pray-not only to assuage my guilt because my religion says you're supposed to pray, but also because talking to God is as much a problem-solving session for me as an act of worship. In those minutes, I decompress and brainstorm. I put my problems and questions before God and ask for answers. I also thank him for any successes I may have had that week.

Religion to me is like a sibling. I don't remember when we first met and I've been taking it for granted for years. I don't remember the first time I visited a mosque. I may have gone as a child for Friday prayers or perhaps it was for a wedding or a funeral. I don't remember the mosque's name or where it was. But I remember the cold as it tingled up the back of my legs, the gentle shock of walking barefoot across a marble floor to a place where I would bow my head in prayer. And I remember the hush occasionally broken by the clinking of gold bracelets, as I stood among a hundred or so other women standing shoulder to shoulder, murmuring praises to Allah. It was submission and it was peaceful. This is an aspect of religion I cherish, an oasis from the busy world outside.

Mezghan

Being a Muslim has helped me become a better person. The teachings of Islam have obviously had a big hand in helping me to understand myself, the purpose of life and the value of being a human and in particular a woman..

On the first day of Eid one year, I chose to go to school after attending the Eid prayer. Most of the Muslim students were absent and my social science teacher asked me to explain Eid and why people fasted for one month. It felt so good to have an opportunity to tell other students about my religion and my culture. After explaining Eid and the motive and purpose of fasting, I noticed that they were surprised to learn good things about a peaceful religion which the media presents so differently.

Maha

I took a summer course at Georgetown University, which has a strong program in Middle Eastern and Arab Studies program. That summer I read Fatima Mernissi's *The Veil and the Male Elite*. It had an enormous impact on my life because it showed me that men have carried out all the exegetical inquiry in Islam. It infuriated me to learn that my religious heritage has been taken away from me, that I have been robbed of such a big part of what it means to be a Muslim and a woman. I also read Nabia Abott's biography of the Prophet's wife Aisha, which explains that early Islam, before the rules were codified, was a much more fluid and dynamic faith. Learning these things was both a wonderful and terrible experience to me as a Muslim woman.

Salima

Grade school is a time when boys have cooties that can be passed onto girls with a touch or a look. But the disease I was being infested with was more serious. Once, in the playground, a group of boys told us that girls were dumb. "You girls will never have power," one of them said. This did not sit well with me. I was determined to find an authoritative argument to counter this. That day I heard a speech by the Imam, in which he spoke of the need for women to educate themselves and to be leaders within society.

The next day I went to school armed with this news that was sure to set the boys straight. I looked them straight in the eyes and said, "I'll see you in twenty years." They all laughed but I walked away with my head held high and proud to be a girl, having found validation about my abilities and purpose from my faith. I realized that I had gained something special from being an Ismaili Muslim girl.

Munira

I was raised an average Canadian child, without any religion preached at home. But I felt there was more to life than what I knew. Once I collected enough information to decide I wanted to practise Islam, I set out a plan as to how my life was going to change inwardly and outwardly. I started slowly to change things about myself. I gradually grew closer to friends who held similar values and created a learning space that would elevate me into a better position.

The Aware

In talking about how we have changed over time as Muslim women, we also thought it would be interesting to know how each of us sees our ideal Muslim women. What does it mean to be a Muslim woman?

Farah

An ideal Muslim woman is a woman who claims to be a follower of Islam, the Prophet and the Qur'an, and depending on the sect you belong to, the Imam. She is someone who is strong but recognizes and is comfortable with her nurturing side also.

Salwa

My ideal Muslim woman is someone who continuously searches for spiritual enlightenment through her rituals and has expressions of servitude to Allah (swt). I admire women who practice their religion through example, whether working in the public sphere or raising a family. I admire women who reach out to all of humanity through compassion, love, honour, faith, justice and education. We are all ambassadors of Islam.

Amber

An ideal Muslim woman is a loving, nurturing, smart, daring, enduring human being who stimulates and provokes discussion and challenges those around her.

Maha

Most of the Muslim women I know are very strong and very authoritative. They exercise a lot of power in their lives, in their families and in the lives of people who love them and whom they love. When I think of Muslim women I think of so many different things, it is difficult to reduce these to a few words.

When I describe myself as a Muslim woman, I am saying that I am part of a specific religious community and proud of it. I am making a statement about myself as a human being. Whether you are male or female, to be Muslim is to undertake certain obligations, not only to God, but also to your fellow human beings. If you are a true Muslim, you should act on behalf of those who can't act for themselves. It means speaking out against injustice. I think your faith obliges you to do that.

Salima

Being a Muslim woman means engaging in life as a process, in which there is guidance and inspiration provided by Islam about how to discover our relationships with the Almighty, each other and the environment. It is about responding to and living among humanity and molding ourselves into agents for change and justice. I think, most importantly, it means living with loving interactions, without judgment and with compassion for all people, especially those who are different from you. We all came from one soul, the Qur'an says, so how can we justify the oppression of anyone? And finally, being Muslim woman means using our intellect, so that we become the intellectual leaders of tomorrow.

Nazneen

For me, a Muslim woman has a strong character and good analytical skills. She can solve problems as a mother or a sister or a friend. She needs to be clear and knowledgeable, especially about her life. I can be submissive at times; there is nothing wrong in saying yes, but women, Muslim or non-Muslim, submit more often than not. I want Muslim women to have more equality because they have greater rights than they realize.

Muslim women have a lot of freedom, but they don't know it. So, examine the holy book and know what your rights are and use them. As Muslim women, we have a lot of impact. We are the ones who are bringing up the new generation. If we don't have answers for ourselves, how will we provide answers for the next generation?

Mezghan

When I think of an ideal Muslim woman, I think of a strong, wise woman who knows her rights and responsibilities; who is open to challenges in life; who knows how to fight for her rights; who believes in herself; who is proud of being a woman and a Muslim; and who is willing to live her life in modesty.

Zaynab

When I say that a Muslim woman is intelligent, I mean she is free-thinking. She does not conform to any one view. She is strong, in that she follows her inner strength and her belief in God and doesn't let anyone tear these down. Even if she is married to a man, she goes by what is right and not by what he says.

Concluding thoughts.

As our discussion reveals, our experiences as Muslim women are wide-ranging. Each woman's unique experience suggests that although gender plays a role in how she experiences Islam, Islam also has an ideal for Muslim women; an ideal that the women have each tried to articulate. One of the key lessons that has come out of this discussion is that a woman's experience of Islam must be an informed one. Knowledge can help foster self-awareness. This self-awareness allows us to experience an Islam that we are responsible for and can expand. Knowledge is the key to awareness, and awareness leads to a humanistic experience of Islam.

To know oneself is to know God.

Majlis al-Bârî
The Evolver

"Cultural work is about naming, who we are as well as who I am, reclaiming the power to name, and to rename as we shift and change, seeing ourselves differently. It allows us to explore who we are and to create new names in the process."

Deborah Barndt

The increasing spread of Western cultural hegemony throughout the world is resulting in a corresponding increase of resistance in the form of nationalist, religious, anti-globalization and cultural movements. Under threat, as people struggle to resist dominant influences, identities become static, limited and reductive, thereby keeping people framed within certain characteristics or categorizations. For example, Muslim and Western identities are pitted against each other. In this binary, each is static and is used to either validate or invalidate the other. Rarely do we ask what we mean by Muslim and "Western" and how those of us living in the West are supposed to negotiate between the two.

One of the problems of the representations of Muslim women is that we are often encapsulated within labels and concepts, our identities defined by others. Women become symbols and objects of community honour, national identity or family status. The reality, however, is that identities are not static. They are fluid and changing over time. With experience and knowledge, our notion of self, what or who we are and how we perceive ourselves and our environment is constantly evolving. We must thus reclaim our power to name ourselves.

It is He Who maketh the stars (as beacons) for you, that ye may guide yourselves, with their help, through the dark spaces of land and sea: We detail Our signs for people who know.

(6:97)

Farah

It is what makes up a person. It's your personality, your culture, your sexual orientation, your political beliefs, everything about you.

Salwa

Identity is something you mold and shape.

Maha

Too often people think of identity as a reductionist label. Identity is truly multifaceted. Most problems arise when you try to reduce identity to a single dimension. I think the most important aspect of identity is that it be flexible and that it is not used to pigeonhole people.

Salima

Identity is an evolving realization of self.

What does Identity mean to you?

Nazneen

I define identity in two ways. Identity tells you about your ancestors, your culture, where you live. The other aspect of identity is what you become at a certain stage in your life.

Munira

Identity is a mixture of who you are and how you present yourself.

Zaynab

Your identity is what your experience is.

What does identity mean to you? The way that our experiences constantly shape our evolving identity can be compared to a flower. With time and nourishment, it will grow into something completely different from its initial form, but still bearing some resemblance to the seed it once was. Keeping this in mind we decided to do some "historical mapping": Going back to moments throughout our lives that have impacted us, helped us grow, learn, deepen our convictions or question them. We shared key moments from our childhood and later years.

Salwa

As a Palestinian, I believe that the seed of consciousness was born in me, whereas with others I believe it is developed. I wasn't born in a refugee camp. I was born in Canada. I had a comfortable though modest upbringing, a good life. I was given a good education and a safe home. I knew I was Muslim and Canadian, but I also knew I was Palestinian. I was always aware of the situation there. Over the years through my university years and onward, this seed of consciousness, this seed of political awareness grew bigger, more intense. I knew I had to deal with my identity. I didn't realize exactly how much my Palestinian-ness was calling out to me, gnawing at me. It's corny to say it, but it was calling to my heart, to my mind, to my soul. I answered it and realized that I had to go back home and see everything with my own eyes and witness first-hand the experiences of Palestinians living under the occupation. I hoped my journey back to my father's homeland, my homeland, would be a cathartic experience. I wanted to go back and see this land that had been filled with so much conflict, suffering and pain for the past fifty-four years. I also knew going back involved responsibilities and an objective to bring back information. This was my duty, not only as a Palestinian but also as a human being, to speak out against oppression and violence.

In Palestine, one thing that struck me was the sense of belonging I felt. I can't exactly explain the feeling, but it's like going into someone's house and immediately feeling at home. I was embraced as one of their own, as part of their family, as part of their community. I felt guilty when I left. I wasn't living under the occupation. And even though I went to show solidarity with them for a short while, leaving them was excruciating, because I have been granted a better

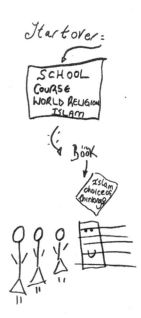

The Evolver

life than them, which doesn't seem fair. My family was driven out of Palestine but built a life in Canada. These families stayed to fight and struggle in the face of hostility and oppression.

Munira

I was born in Canada. My father is from Afghanistan and my mother from Switzerland. When I was growing up, we spent most of our time with Afghan families and so I was familiar with the culture. When I was six my grandfather, who was a religious scholar, visited from Afghanistan. It was the first and only time I met him. He was a kind and peaceful man. My brother and I were very drawn to him. We would sit near him and just watch him. We could not speak to him because of the language but we would still want to be near him and watch him pray. When I think back to that time, I remember it to be a very positive experience of Islam. I had had no previous experience of Islam.

As I grew older I saw more people praying and I tried to understand more about Islam and the purpose of religion and worship. But I kept encountering hypocrisy particularly when culture became entangled with religion. It seemed as though many of the Muslims I met were confusing the two or chose whichever one was more convenient for them at the moment.

Salima

When I was five, my twelve-year-old brother passed away. It was obviously a very sad and difficult time for my family. But something extraordinary happened to me. I was lying in bed one night, shortly after he died, in conversation with God. I suddenly had a realization that this body, this time here, was transitory. A feeling of love overcame me, a feeling that my brother's departure was an act of love, and that he was moving on to the next phase of his journey. I realized that I was a soul, a spiritual being. I began to experience God and love as expansive and all-permeating. Nothing was the same after that. I did not lament my brother's death but instead saw it as a testament to our eternal journey. I had a life altering realization at five. They say that when you are a child you are aware of yourself on a metaphysical level and that as time goes on you begin to lose this awareness. I have not lost it. I thank Allah everyday for this awareness.

My political and social awareness was heightened at nineteen. I decided to teach English in Pakistan. But after a few days there I realized I had not understood what activism truly meant. I met people who had been working their entire lives to challenge systems that limited women's access to education. One woman in her early twenties spoke about her desire to create a world where women did not fear walking the streets and did not live in hopelessness. Such women inspired me. Their dedication forced me to ask myself what I was doing for the betterment of women in my own country and community. I had always been involved in various women-centered activities. But my Pakistan experience shifted my consciousness of what I was doing from a pastime to a life commitment, a life purpose. This helped focus my direction in life. Some of the strongest women I have ever met are in Pakistan: activists, teachers, doctors, NGO directors, and politicians. After meeting them I took a good look at Canada and a good look at my own community and asked what I needed to do here and resolved to do these things.

Amber

My father moved our family to a very small town where we seemed to be the first brown-skinned people they had ever seen and so we faced a lot of racism. They would call us "paki" and tell us to go back to Mecca. What made me really angry is that we are not even from Mecca. If you're going to insult us, at least get it right. One day my brother went outside to play and came back with a bloody nose. I saw him bloodied and crying, and so I went out and up to a snot-nosed kid standing at the edge of the street. I explained to him where we were from and we are Muslim. This was in 1979, when the Iran hostage crisis was taking place and there were many negative images of Muslims everywhere. So, I just spoke to him. I am sure I was screaming a little bit, too. But after that, things improved. We got to know the kids. The boy ended up being my brother's best friend.

When thinking about our identity let us not only look within but let us also look around us.

The Evolver

Mezghan

I am tired of being identified by others and through others. I am an Afghan but I don't want people to know me through the Taliban and what they did in Afghanistan-not because I deny what they did but because I am not a terrorist or Taliban. I don't necessarily agree with their philosophies, nor do I think the Taliban are even Afghans. They are in fact invaders from neighbouring countries.

I want people to know my beliefs, talents, capabilities and, through them, that they know me. They can't know me from what other Muslim women do or what other Afghan Muslim women are like. Identity is what makes each person unique. I think one's beliefs, practices, likes and dislikes, and abilities to challenge and survive make up her identity.

How does the past influence the present?

And how can the present help us explore the past?

Maha

Have you heard of Nusrat Fateh Ali Khan? He is a Pakistani qawwal (devotional singer) who died a few years ago. He sang qawwalis, which are basically poems in praise of the Prophet and God set to music. There is one song, "Yeh jo halka, halka saroor" (soft intoxication) that my father swears is not meant to be a song to God. He insists it's a secular love song, even though it contains religiously oriented phrases. I don't agree. Every time I hear this qawwali, I feel that this person is obviously singing to God, and God is responding back to him, saying you should thank me for creating you and endowing you with the ability to create this poetry. I guess it could be interpreted as a love song because the qawwal is singing about love for an individual. He even talks about being lovesick. But to me it still seems that this person is singing to God. I think it is such a beautiful metaphor, relating to God as a lover. It reminded me that God is love. I think we tend to forget that idea and instead focus on other aspects of God. God has love for us and that love should be reflected in the love that we have for each other. The very first time I heard this qawwali, I felt joy, I felt bliss, I felt in my early teens a real sense of peace and serenity and, most of all, I felt a real sense of God's love for me and for humanity.

Farah

Growing up as a Muslim woman has been difficult and challenging at times. I would dread it when Saddam Hussein, the Middle East, terrorism, oppressed women or the *Satanic Verses* were brought up in class for discussion. I felt a burning anger inside me; I desperately wanted to shout out that Western perception of Muslims is tainted, that Islam as a religion does not preach violence, that the media rarely give an accurate picture of Muslims or the situation in the Middle East. But instead I remained silent, out of fear that I would be looked upon as a terrorist, or a brainwashed, oppressed woman, and that I would thereafter be the one looked upon to give the Muslim perspective and be bombarded with counterarguments that I might not be able to argue against. So I sat silently in class while ignorant people had discussions about Muslims and the religion I knew and practised. As I grew older, I found the courage to speak up, though throughout high school these discussions often revolved around politics.

When I was in university, in the women's studies faculty, I found that discussions about Muslim women centered around the oppression they suffer and the violations of human rights they endure under Islam (unlike in the Western world where women are treated with utmost respect and have equal standing to men in society). It seemed that somehow it had been decided that the universal symbol for Islam was a woman wearing hijab or burqa. It still made me angry, but I felt better equipped to handle the situation.

Nazneen

In my first year of college, most of the people in my class were white. We were asked to do a presentation and I chose to do mine on Pakistani weddings. During my presentation people started bombarding me with questions and at that moment I realized my role as a Muslim in this society. They asked me questions such as, Can a guy get married seven times? Clearly their information was coming from the media. I quickly realized that I had to do something to counter this misinformation and it was not going to be easy. I answered every question in detail. Whether they believed me or not was irrelevant, at least they heard a different story from my end. As a Muslim, I have to maintain my identity but also have to clarify misunderstandings about our religion.

Childhood
Muslims
Ismailis — everyone else
Liberal esoteric
US
Not "those" kinds of muslims
feeling like I should seperate myself
making divisions myself
(them "other")

In our discussions about identity and how we are perceived and treated, we also felt it was important to talk about our experiences of racism. As women of colour we are subjected to interlocking systems of oppression based on race, class, gender and religious and sexual orientation.

Racism defined:

Racism is the exercise of power, whether intended or not, by the dominant racial group over others, of different skin colour and racial heritage. Racism may be expressed systemically (policies, procedures, etc), or through individual acts (racial slurs, racist jokes, lynchings, etc). Racism whether individual or systemic influences social beliefs, stereotypes and assumptions about people. These are usually unexamined beliefs about the inherent inferiority of people of colour and aboriginal people.

What systems and structures perpetuate racism?

Government, media, educational systems, corporations, families, communities, religious institutions.

Who are those in power and influence and shape these systems and put forth particular perspectives?

The dominant group, who has power in the form of money and positions of influence in society.

Within the Canadian context?

White, male, Anglo-Saxon, Christian, middle and upper class, heterosexual.

How is racism perpetuated? Some examples

History is told from a Eurocentric perspective.

The media characterize minoritized groups (i.e. Muslims are terrorists, Blacks are criminals, Japanese are studious, etc.).

The educational system (teachers, administration, etc.) does not reflect the diversity of students and peoples.

Minoritized groups are not in positions to have influence on policy and ideology.

Our institutions do not reflect moniritized groups in their make-up.

Stories of racism.

Mezghan

When I was in Afghanistan, I faced a lot of racism and discrimination. I belong to a province in central Afghanistan called Bamyan. We have a distinctive physical appearance and so our race is considered inferior, because we could rarely obtain important jobs or high positions, or places in the medical university. Even if someone from our race had very high marks, she did not manage to meet the requirements and was not eligible to become a doctor. On the exam paper you were asked to indicate your race. The person who graded the paper made sure she checked the race first and gave marks accordingly. Living in Pakistan, I faced racism too. We were looked down upon as Afghan refugees. In everyday life there were numerous experiences of racism.

When I first began volunteering at a hospital here in Canada, the person whom I was supposed to work with asked me where I was from. Then he asked if I was Muslim and I told him I was, even though I knew there was no reason he needed to know this. Then he asked, "Where is your burqa?" He was shocked to find an Afghan girl without a burqa.

The Evolver

Zaynab

Being lighter skinned and female, according to the stereotype of Asian women, we are considered great nurses and great housewives or passive, fragile exoticized objects. I have fought to resist such labeling.

Nazneen

I can relate to that. People put you in a box. We come from everywhere but as brown-skinned people we are put in the same box. My colour is all they see.

Salima

I grew up in what I now call the Indian Ghetto, yet most of my teachers were not people of colour. I found that most of my experiences of racism came from teachers and some other minoritized groups, that were new to this country but had the privilege of having white skin. I remember one guy who felt that all of us brown-skinned people could be grouped into one category called "pakis." Did he ever harass us. He would follow us around taunting us with this term. Finally, one day I stepped up to him and gave him an equally offensive response. I was not proud of myself. I had reverted to a racial slur out of frustration, but it did not appear to affect this guy. He just looked at me and walked away singing "paki." How frustrating. We complained to the teacher and we were told to ignore him. As if he had the right to infest public space with his foul language and we had to accommodate him by ignoring it. I was very upset. Apparently, we were the problem and not he because we could not ignore him. Talk about being livid and feeling completely unsafe in school.

Munira

Whenever I'm with a group of white Canadians and they ask where I am from, I tell them I'm Canadian and they say, "No really, where are you from?" They do not expect me to be Canadian born. On the flip side, if I am with a group of Afghans I tend to say that I am Afghani because I know that is what they want to hear. They do not want to hear that I am Canadian born or half Swiss or half Afghan.

Nazneen

At my workplace, it is obvious that my company does not hire brown-skinned people, or women for high management positions. The dominant positions are filled by white men. I always expected that my race would be a barrier at work and to some degree it has been, but my class has had an interesting impact. I believe that in the perception of management I come from a different class, or better class than most other immigrants who work there and so I find that I am treated better than they are. People notice my privileges, and I don't feel good about it.

Zaynab

What really gets me is this gradation in skin color. For example, you may be considered light-skinned brown or dark-skinned brown, and it seems that lighter skin is always preferred. This is obvious when you hear things such as, Don't marry someone who is too dark, or Light skin is beautiful.

Salima

That reiterates for me the reverence given to the colour white. There are associations that we make with colours. For example, white represents purity, black represents evil. Measures of beauty are based on the ideal in society. In North America, the women who are considered ideally beautiful are not women of colour. The same is true in other parts of the world, especially within India and elsewhere, reverence of whiteness is a legacy of the colonial past when "whiteness" was forced on people as better, cleaner, more beautiful and more civilized. And now with globalization and the Western mass media infiltrating every part of the globe, these same dominant images are being perpetuated.

Final thoughts.

Reflecting on our experiences gives us a better sense of who we are and how we got here. Identifying with something or someone larger can give us a sense of belonging and connection. However, when identity is determined by simplistic definitions of gender, race, class, religion, and culture, the complexities of who we are are lost, along with the ability to reach deeper levels of self-awareness as individuals or groups. Unless identities are seen to be expansive and transforming with time, they will be used as tools to oppress. Naming ourselves and our lives is an on-going process that allows us to be agents of change.

I will not be the paint on your canvas.

Majlis al-Mujîb
The Responsive

Stereotypes are essential to producing "Otherness" and inferiority. The creation of the Other is achieved by reducing people and concepts to one-dimensional categories. For example, Western world = progressive; Third World = backward; Westerners = non-violent; Muslims = terrorists. Such categorizations produce perceptions that are used to legitimize imbalances of power. We need to examine the effects of these reductions in order to reclaim our power to represent ourselves.

The media have played a vital role in producing reductive images and notions of marginalized groups. We have begun to critically examine these media representations by evaluating their messages about Muslim women and Islam. We deconstructed popular ideas and images through "ad-busting." Ad-busting is a means of challenging the messages in media advertisements by creating responses or alternative messages.

Finally, we examined how Islam and the West are conceptualized. Complete rejection of the West and Western values is not realistic or helpful, living in the West or, with globalization, living anywhere. Thus, we examined ideas, values and ways of life that we take from the Western world that don't contradict the values and ethics of Islam.

"Representation is a complex business and especially when dealing with difference', it engages feelings, attitudes, and emotions and it mobilizes fears and anxieties..."
(Hall, 226:1997)

As a group we faced many challenges and tensions in speaking about these issues. Representing ourselves is not an easy task because we want to present different ideas and perhaps even convey different messages at times. The veil, modesty and sexuality were particularly contentious topics, causing some people to leave the group and making others feel attacked and unsafe. In the end, we concluded that processes such as these are not perfect and topics such as these are not easy to talk about. Our commitment to work through these difficulties deepened through the sessions, because we knew this was the only way to build bridges and to expand ourselves as individuals and communities.

"Who out there is creating a worthwhile Muslim Identity?"
(Choudhury, 5, 2000)

The Responsive

The media have played a significant role in the misrepresentation of Islam and Muslims. We need to look at who the media are and why they have such influence in shaping the perceptions of a group made up of over one billion.

What do we mean by the media? The media are:

disseminators of information

venues for knowledge-exchange and -sharing

socializing tools for society

creators of archetypes of peoples and cultures and in turn shapers of our perception of these groups

sources of entertainment

mirrors of particular aspects of social interactions and structures

How has the Muslim and Islamic archetype developed and fared within the media? What are they saying about "us"?

Mezghan

Islam breeds terrorism, Muslims are ignorant and Muslim women are oppressed.

Salima

Guess who I am talking about. They look "different." They carry around a book everywhere they go. Their God's name starts with an A. Their women are covered in veils and their men flex their muscles by keeping women under their thumbs. Anybody?

Islam has become a fossilized symbol. Clearly, the message in the media (news, movies, etc.) has been that Islam is evil and finds expression through its fanatical followers. Muslims are undemocratic; we have no concept of rights and freedoms; we have a poor sense of fashion if we are covered all the time; we are uneducated; we are territorial savages; and the list goes on.

The most damaging evidence against Muslims is their treatment of women. It is a backward religion that forces its women to cover up and unleashes deplorable violence on those who do not comply with its very orthodox and rigid prescriptions. This is Islam according to the "reliable" and "unbiased" authorities of the Western media. I am tired of this save-the-world-from-the-Muslims rhetoric that is thrown around by the very self-interested mainstream media. Aren't you?

Amber

Yes I am. In North America at least, "Muslims are the barbarians at the gate. Muslims are from the stone age. Muslims are medieval. Muslims are to be feared. Muslims have weapons. Muslims who have weapons are not to be trusted. The West must band together and fight the Muslims." There are good Muslims and there are bad Muslims.

What they don't realize is that they're missing a really big story. Why is Islam the fastest-growing religion in the world? What's the big attraction? What does Islam do that makes an average John Walker Lindh chuck his life in San Francisco and go to Afghanistan? It's not roti. It's the vision of respect, security and something else, presumably. It got mangled along the way and mixed in with guns and war, but surely it started off pure.

Nazneen

I came to Canada in 1992. I remember the Oklahoma City bombing. Without any evidence, the president of the United States announced on international television that it appeared that Muslim terrorists did this. Sure, later they apologized, but how can people in power say such things without evidence?

So, how does power play into this? Who owns the media? Whose interests are presented?

'The mass media serve as a system for communicating messages and symbols to the general populace. It is their function to amuse, entertain, and inform, and to inculcate individuals with the values, beliefs and codes of behaviour that will integrate them into the institutional structures of the larger society...in countries where the levers of power are in the hands of the state bureaucracy, the monopolistic control over the media, often supplemented by official censorship, makes it clear that the media serve the ends of the dominant elite."

(Noam Chomsky 2002, 1)

The media is owned by:

There are nine transnational media conglomerates:

Disney, AOL Time Warner, Viacom (owner of CBS), News Corporation, Bertelsmann, General Electric (owner of NBC), Sony, AT&T-Liberty Media, and Vivendi Universal.

(Noam Chomsky 2002, X111)

Why has the message been such?

Zaynab

It's fear of the unknown. For instance, some racists ignorantly say that all blacks are criminals. Well, I can say that all serial killers are white!

The fact is, there are good and bad in all races and cultures. You cannot lump everyone together because of the few rotten apples that are constantly portrayed by the media. If the media were to portray the goodness in Islam, people would not be interested. It is human nature to crave drama. What are the most popular books or movies? Ones with sex, drama and action. In the US, because they are predominantly Christian and their laws are rooted in Christianity, we as Muslims are always portrayed as the Other.

Amber

I think it's lack of knowledge. I don't want to believe that educated, intelligent journalists buy into the US claim that Muslim terrorists are a threat to the entire world. That said, once the Cold War ended, the West needed a new bad guy and, look, here comes Islam around the corner. The fear of Islam that exists in the West goes back 1100 years, that kind of fear doesn't just disappear, even if it is 2003 and we are politically correct.

Salima

Can we really answer the question of why without looking at who owns the media.? Over-representation of one group will inevitably influence what trickles down to the consumers of media. And there is an over-representation, not just in numbers but also in perspectives. When the media is in the hands of a few, the perspectives they offer will be limited. Who are these people in positions of power? White, upper-class, heterosexual, Christian, Anglo-Saxon, males. Do you see yourself in this picture?

Maha

According to the Canadian Oxford Dictionary Fundamentalism: Strict maintenance of ancient or fundamental doctrines of any religion. Esp Islam. Fundamentalist n & adj

Terrorism: the systematic employment of violence and intimidation to coerce a government or community, esp. into acceding to specific political demands.

Part of the problem is rooted in the colonial past and its legacy of fearing the Other, seen as a savage, blood-thirsty killer. I think politics are a big reason as well. When the Cold War ended, the Muslims became the new bogeymen. Within Western imagination and political discourse, Muslims replaced the Soviets. Afghanistan is an excellent example. These militants (Osama Bin Laden and the Mujahedeen) are the way they are because the US funded them in the war against the Soviets. They thought that this force of zealous, religious young men would be potentially useful in driving the Soviets out. This is a monster the US created. Once the Soviets left, these men remained with American money, CIA training, and US-purchased weapons. Look what happened.

Certain ideas and concepts about Islam permeate media rhetoric. We looked at how, "fundamentalism," "terrorism" and "jihad" are presented in the media. It becomes clear with even the most superficial examination that these terms are used to define Muslims as violent and to narrowly define Islam and its beliefs. We explored our varied definitions of these terms.

Zaynab

When I hear "terrorism," the first thing that comes to my mind is the US. What do most people think of? Because of ignorance and, of course the role of the media, they think of Muslims and Islam. People need to take a good look at American foreign policy and its forms of fundamentalism. How is it that the US can rape and take away people's land and freedom and instill fear and no one says anything? Isn't that terrorism? Isn't that fundamentalism?

The Responsive

Munira

I believe that I'm a fundamentalist. Not in the way that our society describes it but in the real definition of the word, meaning, following the fundamentals of my faith, going to the roots of my religion and representing its authenticity. Unfortunately in today's society the word "terrorist" has become synonymous with "Muslim." Therefore if Muslims are defending their land they are considered terrorists rather than freedom fighters. I don't support people committing violence. But when I examine the situation of Palestinians, I see people who have not been treated humanely or fairly even in the most basic ways, such as being provided with distribution of water, housing and employment. I see people who are ignored by the world and are left with few ways to defend themselves.

Nazneen

Taking things literally is fundamentalism, and taking violent action based on those fundamental beliefs can be terrorism.

Farah

When people resort to violence, it is because they are afraid and not open minded. From the point of view of such people, their interpretation of Islam is the only way to practise and any other interpretation is a threat to their beliefs. So they spread their word by instilling fear. Due to a few radical people, Islam in its entirety is looked upon as a violent, barbaric religion, which we know couldn't be further from the truth.

Maha

It's very dangerous to simply dismiss fundamentalists as crazy. If people are turning to a particular social movement in such numbers you have to ask why. Obviously that movement is fulfilling a certain need. In places such as Pakistan there has been a definite increase in membership of religious groups. I believe this is a consequence of people's extreme discontent with the state. The hope and aspirations that people had in 1947 when the country was created, that they would have a better life, that this was a country for Muslims, lie in the dust.

The religious organizations have agendas of their own, but the fact that people are turning to them in such great numbers is purely an indication of how frustrated they are. If these religious groups are tapping into people's existing religious beliefs and telling them that it is possible to have a utopian state, that it is possible to lead a life where you can live with respect, that it is possible for you to educate your children, it is possible for you to live in security and have your basic needs met, then of course people will be interested in what these groups are saying and doing.

For example, entire sections of Tunis have been transformed by fundamentalist groups. These groups have cleaned up neighbourhoods, made healthcare available, and so forth. I completely agree that the fundamentalist configuration of women is problematic, wrong, and dangerous, but I think it's equally dangerous to dismiss them as the lunatic fringe. These groups have come about and grown as a result of specific political and social changes that could have been foreseen and prevented.

Everyone talks about terrorist activities but the media do not examine why these activities exist. No one analyzes why people feel so backed into a corner they believe they have no other option but terrorism.

Salwa

I agree with Maha's point that there is a serious need to critically examine why acts of violence are taking place in certain parts of the world. If you look at Palestine and ask why there is a surge of participation in Islamic organizations there, perhaps part of the answer lies in the fact that their needs and aspirations are being acknowledged and met through these organizations.

What frustrates me the most is the use of semantics in all this. Yesterday's "freedom fighter" is today's "terrorist." When does a Palestinian's right to resist occupation, a right that is enshrined in international law, become a terrorist act? I am fully aware that in today's political arena, any endorsement of a Palestinian's right to resist occupation is tantamount to supporting terrorism. This frightens me because it distracts us from the true reason for this conflict. The conflict exists because of the Israeli occupation of Palestinian land. Palestinians have no other alternative but to resist occupation until their homeland is liberated.

The Responsive

In the current climate, it is extremely troubling for me to witness Israel's "war on terrorism" justifying the escalation of crimes against the Palestinian people. I pray that people start critically examining what is happening in the world and see the true picture.

Mezghan

If you are rigid and inflexible in your beliefs and choose to interpret words in the Qur'an or the Bible, for example, literally, then that could be called fundamentalism.

Consider a tree in a storm. If the tree is flexible, it bends with the wind and then straightens again. However, if the tree is rigid and inflexible, then it resists and there is a clash between the wind and the tree. Likewise, I think, a clash between two rigid and inflexible beliefs or policies is terrorism. It contains violence and destruction.

Salima

Fundamentalism is a word that is thrown around quite freely and dangerously with respect to Islam. There are many ways in which fundamentalism can be defined. That is probably one of the most important things to point out, because at present fundamentalism seems to have only one meaning, Islam. In fact, fundamentalism, as a term and concept, found its inception in Christianity in the early twentieth century as a way to resist the over-secularization of American society. Fundamentalism is also a way of espousing very literal views and beliefs about people and the world. I see that fundamentalism in political discourse, in particular in discourse that justifies violence by claiming that it is a necessary and noble form of self-preservation. Dominant American political ideas are the most obvious example of fundamentalism but another example that stands out is India, where Hinduism is tightly interwoven into national identity, thereby alienating all other groups. Politicians, in particular the BJP (Bharatiya Janata Party) use such rhetoric to plant seeds of division and hatred and then water them with continual attacks against anything that does not support their brand of ideology. Fundamentalism is not peculiar to Islam or Muslims.

Amber

I'm so tired of seeing the word "fundamentalism" used in front of "Muslim" in newspaper stories. When I think of fundamentals, I think of the basics and there's nothing wrong with going back to the basics. It's become a bad word, a way to criticize aspects of Islam, and that really bothers me.

Jihad: What does it means?

In the media "jihad" is translated as "holy war." The precise translation of "jihad" is "struggle." There are two kinds of jihad:

The first is Jihad Al-Akbar, the greater struggle. This is the internal struggle that every human being faces to be a better person, to challenge the temptations to lie, cheat, cause harm to others, and so on.

The other jihad is the external struggle to protect the physical self, community or country when attacked or threatened. In this jihad there are rules that must be followed. Some of the rules include: not destroying property, not harming women, children or the elderly, not harming plants, animals, trees, etc.

What can we do to challenge this situation?

Educate people and attain positions of power

Munira

With everything that is going on in today's world, I believe the best thing I can do to challenge the messages and images that the public receives about Islam through the media is to educate them. In order to do that I must first educate myself and understand Islam as much as I can. I try and focus on issues that this society has trouble understanding, such as women's roles, the right to education, duties towards our families and current events in Islamic countries. Whenever I can help clear up a misconception I feel that I am helping Islam and the next generation of Muslims.

The Responsive

Farah

As more women and Muslims get into the media and into positions of power, I think things will slowly improve. And I think little by little things are changing. Educating ourselves is the key. We really need to get into those positions where we can influence. I say, become MPs, writers, and CEOs, whatever it takes.

Salwa

Speak up and speak loudly. Not only is it our duty as Muslims to educate others, it is our duty to speak out against injustices and untruths. We must not be afraid to speak when it comes to defending ourselves as Muslims. We can help the organizations that aim at empowering Muslims in Canada in the fields of politics, media, and social-activism.

The need for role models and appropriate representatives

Nazneen

I think we need more role models. Asma Jehangir, a lawyer in Pakistan, is one woman whom I see as a role model. Rifat Hassan, a scholar, is another. But these women are not here in North America. We need representatives here. The Urdu saying, "paralikhe unpar," in Urdu comes to mind. This describes people who have received an education but still act ignorantly. I sometimes wonder what the point of all this education is if we can't do good things and serve as role models for others.

Salima

We need to be more vocal, to get out there and provide more stories. Let's use the power and influence we do have to create these opportunities for ourselves. We need to examine and unlearn the information we are fed and expose its problems. I think the educational system needs to play a big role in this. Let's demand curricula that include Islamic history and philosophy. Let's hear stories about great Islamic thinkers. We need to find a completely different way of seeing certain things and we need to teach our children to do the same. It is vitally important that we provide tools for the public to scrutinize and challenge information they are receiving.

Adbusting images of Muslim women and messages about Islam

We decided to confront some of the media representations in magazine ads and transform the messages they were giving.

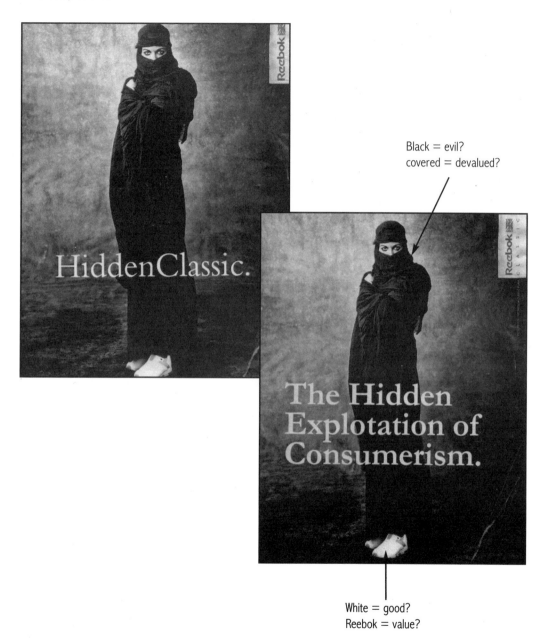

Muslim Women?

We examined loaded terms, such as, West and Islam and how Muslim women are portrayed and defined in the West. Through this exercise we deconstructed some of the myths implicit in the stereotypes and thereby challenged simplistic dichotomies. Next, we identified what we have gained both from Islam and Canada. We realize that our descriptions are also loaded and have implications that depend on one's race, class and gender. Note the similarities in both lists, suggesting that both Islam and the West are not dichotomies.

Where did these stereotypes and myths come from?

How can we change them?

Islam	West
Women = no rights	Women = rights
submissive	Liberal
Covered	exposed (revealed)
Oppressed	Free
Uneducated	Educated
Dumb	Intelligent
Violent	non-Violent
Dirty	Sparkling clean
Uncivilized	Civilized
Homogenous	Multicultural
Sexist	Non sexist
Asexual	Virgin by choice
Traditional	Celebrates tradition
Backward (primitive)	Modern
Ahistorical	History
Technologically inept	Technologically advanced
Passive	Aggressive
Liars, cheaters	Trustworthy, honest
Warmongers (terrorists)	Peace makers
Undemocratic	Democratic

The Responsive

Trying to create more "positive" and "real" representations of Muslim women and Islam can be difficult, especially because we each represent different traditions and interpretations of Islam. For example, the hijab was seen as a symbol of liberation and Muslim identity to some, and also a symbol that excludes the millions of Muslim women who don't relate to the hijab. Discussing our views about sexual orientation illuminated our differences as well, in terms of what and who our Islam includes and excludes.

Islam	West (Canada)
Respect for women	Education
Spirituality	Opportunity
Balance of life between spiritual and material	Right to make own decision
	Multicultural
Peace	High standards of living
Strong value system	Some protection for women
Ethics on how to live responsibly	Health care
Practical approach to life	Freedom to travel
Importance of eduction and intellectual search	Seniors benefits
connections between humans and environment	Social assistance
Strong scientific and philosophical contributions	Freedom of speech
Art and architecture	Religious freedom
Community development	
Social justice	
Commitment to family and community	

How do we create a society where these are the lived experience of all people everyday?

99

Our discussion about modesty and the hijab.

Many women felt the hijab was a symbol of a Muslim woman's spiritual progression and a sign of true modesty

Nazneen

I remember one experience in Canada with Muslim women wearing the hijab. They implied I am not a Muslim because I am not in hijab. They made comments to me and my sister such as, "You go to clubs I am sure." I don't go to clubs but even if I did that wouldn't make me a bad person. But that's the kind of image some Muslim women have. Actually, those women gave me a lot to think about. I learned that I don't want to be a Muslim like them, people who distort my religion.

Maha

It's important to challenge the images that others have of us. It's also important to break down the images we have of one another. I think that a lot of women who wear the hijab do so as a step in their spiritual journey. They feel that it symbolizes a major part of their faith. But I think that there are many Muslim women who will never wear the hijab, and that is also a choice.

Zaynab

It occurred to me when I met a Muslim sister who was completely covered that I felt completely naked.

Farah

When women claim that those Muslim women who choose not to wear the hijab are confused about modesty or are simply not ready to wear the hijab, I feel outraged. Maybe I feel that by wearing the hijab I will feel oppressed. But I am not going to tell you I think you are oppressed because you wear the hijab. And I don't want to be told I am not ready or that I am confused, because I am not confused in the least. I know exactly what kind of Muslim I am. The fact is that I will never wear the hijab, because to me that does not represent Islam or a good Muslim woman.

The Responsive

Zaynab

I would one day like to wear the hijab and that is a personal choice. I have a problem with wearing a hijab, because this society tends to view Muslim women in hijab as oppressed. My question to Muslim women is: Are you wearing it because you want to or because you were told to wear it? It is important to be a strong Muslim woman and to be able to make choices without caring what others think. If people were to see any of us on the street without the hijab they wouldn't even know we were Muslim. But this is my hope, that every woman has a choice

Farah

Last week, when we were discussing the hijab, some of the women who have chosen to wear hijab raised the question of why others don't make the same choice as they. Someone asked if these women don't feel they are good enough to dress modestly. But maybe I feel I can dress modestly without covering my head and every inch of my body. There are different definitions of modesty, and that needs to be recognized. Maybe I feel I am too good to cover myself up completely-I am proud of who I am and would feel very uncomfortable if I had to cover my head at all times. It becomes problematic when people judge other people's "goodness" and their faith and impose their beliefs on others.

Munira

We also follow different Islamic rules and perhaps in some sects it's not compulsory. The definition of modesty varies between women and the sect they belong to.

Salima

Actually, I think that the argument regarding sect should also be examined, because I know that many of the women who have written about the hijab, such as Laila Ahmed and Riffat Hassan, are Sunni women who discuss a very particular historical development of the hijab, and talk about the hijab having little Qur'anic backing. So when we are talking about sects, you may be right about the general understanding within a particular tradition, but women within those very traditions are doing some interesting work that challenges this understanding. This is in no way meant to discredit any woman who chooses to wear hijab, but I think that we need to be careful about sweeping generalizations.

Last week we were ad-busting an image of a Muslim woman wearing hijab. I said this image does not represent me. A woman wearing full hijab may say, "This is about my choice, about my rights," but for me it's simply not representative of me or most Muslim women I know. This is not an issue of rights or choices. It is an issue of one image being used to represent all Muslim women, and that's highly problematic.

Munira

I was struck when you said that that picture does not represent Islam. When I am at work, I have to explain to people that I don't shake hands with men and that a Muslim woman, regardless of whether she is wearing the hijab or not, may not want to shake a man's hand. I always try to let people know that there are differences in the way people practise Islam. Much of my time is spent focusing on Muslim women wearing hijab in the workplace, because that is what I am faced with. However, I also realize that sisters not wearing hijab, for whatever reason, face struggles as well.

Salima

I didn't say that it (hijab) doesn't represent Islam. I feel strongly that it cannot be the sole representation of Islam and of women as followers of the faith. This representation dismisses the many identities of Muslim women. And when the West uses the hijabed woman to represent and depict Muslim women, it further homogenizes Muslim women, even those who wear the hijab, by sending the message that Muslim women who wear the hijab reflect particular values and live out particular gender roles.

There is another danger of homogeneity. Let's take for example those women who do believe in covering themselves. If we took a survey of Muslim women across the world, we would find that Muslim women cover themselves differently. Some wear the hijab, some wear the abay (full-body cover), some just put a dupatta (piece of cloth) over their heads. Such differences in covering could stem from differences in interpretation. In my reading, the Qur'an does not ask women to cover their heads. It asks for modesty. As for whether or not one should cover, I think that is a personal decision. At times there is forcible veiling, which happens within some Muslim communities, and then there is forcible unveiling, which happened in the case of Iran under the Shah, and most recently in Turkey. Dogmatism is dogmatism, whether it is in the name of "Westernization" or "Islamicization." There is no compulsion in religion.

Salwa

I believe that the hijab is a personal relationship between a Muslimah and Allah (swt). It is a sign of taqwa (piety) and imaan. The Qur'an says, "Say to the believing man that they should lower their gaze and guard their modesty; that will make for greater purity for them; and Allah is well acquainted with all that they do. And say to the believing women that they should lower their gaze and guard their modesty; and that they should not display their beauty and ornaments except what must ordinarily appear thereof; that they should draw their veils over their bosoms and not display their beauty except to their husbands, their fathers…" (Surah 24: 30-31).

It is clear from these verses that modesty is required of both the male and the female. But I believe that modesty is not merely covering one's head with a scarf or covering one's body with loose clothing. It is how we present ourselves to others in public, in the way we behave, in the way we speak, in the way we choose to represent ourselves. But each Muslim woman is free to make her own interpretation.

I fundamentally believe in the hijab, and hope one day, inshallah, to wear it. However, how I carry myself now without the hijab in no way negates the level of piety and faith I have for my religion and for God. When I complete my spiritual elevation and wear the hijab, I know that with it will come great responsibility, not only religious but also political and social. I will be identifiable as a "visible" Muslim woman, an identity that will have to find a place among other Muslim women.

Mezghan

What is the real purpose of hijab?

1. Modesty: full cover, half cover, no cover

2. Protection, security

3. Avoiding sin

While I was in Afghanistan, before the Mujahedeen and then the Taliban took over parts of Afghanistan, it was a choice to wear the hijab. I lived in Kabul, where most women chose not to wear it. When the Mujahedeen came to power, women were required to wear a veil, to cover their heads (and exposed body parts). The requirement was not very strict. However, when the Taliban invaded Afghanistan, women were forced to wear burqa.

When my family fled to Pakistan, we lived in the city of Peshawar. There, too, women observed hijab. I think this was mainly because of the dirty comments of the men walking on the streets.

After coming to Canada, I chose not to wear the hijab, because I did not feel as insecure as before, when I would draw attention if I did not wear it. I felt free, secure and in peace. Now I am not wearing hijab; however, I think I am observing hijab, in a way: through my behaviour, my actions, my speech, my dress and everything I do. Not wearing a veil does not necessarily make me "immodest." And wearing a veil alone does not make one modest. I am sure most of you, if not all, would agree with me. If a woman wears the hijab and does "sinful" things, is she a modest woman? Not really. What if a woman does not wear the hijab but lives a clean life, is she modest? I think so. I'm not saying that women wearing hijab do sinful things. I think to be a modest woman, hijab is not a requirement. We could be modest even without wearing it. But I do respect hijab, as well as those wearing it.

Our discussion about sexual orientation.

Munira

Last week was very interesting to me. For the most part, since I have started practising I have mostly been involved with the Shia Ithnashari and Sunni communities. It has been very interesting meeting all the sisters and sharing our struggles. When I first spoke with Salima, I assumed I would be involved with a group of sisters who were practising similarly. I am happy to be a part of this group because I believe that it is important to support a project that will help others understand Islam and who Muslim women are. However, I did have issues with exploring topics such as sexual orientation, because my definition of Islam is very clear on that. I was worried that I was getting involved with a project that was going to promote and present Islam as a religion that approves of homosexuality.

Zaynab

I don't necessarily agree with homosexuality as Islamic, but as a woman, I think that people have the right to live their lives as they want. But if one chooses Islam, then homosexuality is something that is contradictory to what Islam says and they should think about that. I guess everybody has different sides to them.

Salima

Not to include people within Islam because of their sexual orientation is ridiculous to me. That is not the Islam I live, which is loving and all-embracing. Whether the Qur'an has stipulated that homosexuality is "allowed" or is "correct" is something that should be carefully explored. But at the end of the day, the answer to that question is irrelevant to me. This is personal and something you and God will talk about. What does anybody accomplish by creating an Islam that is hateful or in denial about people's differences? How is it any more Islamic to discriminate and in many cases hate or alienate people from their faith, their community, and sometimes even their God?

Mezghan:

I wonder if your sexual orientation would affect your relationship to God? Will God refuse to be your God if you are a homosexual? If so, perhaps God is "prejudiced."

If even one person dies through injustice humanity has failed its self.

Majlis al-'Adl

The Just

O ye who believe! stand out firmly for justice, as witnesses to Allah, even as against yourselves, or your parents, or your kin, and whether it be (against) rich or poor: for Allah can best protect both. Follow not the lusts (of your hearts), lest ye swerve, and if ye distort (justice) or decline to do justice, verily Allah is well-acquainted with all that ye do.

(4:135)

As we have discussed at length, in the general Western perception of Islam, women are defined as the victims of an oppressive, dogmatic faith. Dialogue with Muslim women about their experiences in their faith and their individual communities has for the most part been nonexistent. We have strived to change that here and in the process tried to come to a deeper level of awareness about what role Islam plays in our lives. But we have also attempted to reveal some aspects of Islam that we are still trying to understand, reiterating that Islam is a journey and that we are in a process of learning and strengthening our relationships to each other and to God. As seekers, our journeys illuminate the dynamic processes of our intellectual and spiritual search.

We also talked about how Islam informs social justice. Notions of justice, equity, environmental and social responsibility, community, and service to humankind are ethical premises in Islam that are reiterated both in history and in the Qur'an. Islam offers guidance about how to build a humanistic existence, one in which we are in harmony not only with each other, but also with the earth, the universe and ultimately God.

Lastly, each woman shared her experience of resistance and activism in challenging the present and in changing the future.

The Just

What does Islam mean to you?

Munira

Islam means using the Prophet's words and guidance as revealed to him by God and following and submitting to that guidance, which describes the best way of life. Take for example the line, "Bismillahir Rahmanir Rahim..." What does it mean and what goes through your mind as you recite it? Many people may just pray and repeat the words that are prescribed, but I believe we should reflect on what we are reciting during our prayers. Islam is a code of ethics for our lives, sent to us by our creator who knows us best.

Nazneen

Islam is a very practical religion. It gives you freedom, but those in power want to keep the control in their hands, so they manipulate Islam according to their needs. I find the meaning of religion in spiritual poetry. The mystics talk about the relationship between you and God. You can share anything with God. That's my Islam. You don't need a Moulvi (religious leader) or even your parents; they can guide you, but it's your own adventure to discover. Islam is an adventure that never ends and everyone finds his or her own way. It's like the sky: it has no boundaries.

But the world in which we are living has set so many boundaries that we are moving away from the essence of Islam. People are forgetting their relationship with God. The Qur'an says that humans are "Ashraful makhluqat," which means we are superior to everything God has created in the world because we are given the ability to reason and think. God has given us the tools to make good decisions and using these tools is what Islam means to me.

Islam ~ loving submission to the will of God.

Zaynab

Islam means totally submitting to the Almighty, not through prayer alone but also through practice. I realize this is subject to interpretation, but to me, the Almighty encompasses everything in life, on every level, spiritual, physical, mental and emotional. Islam is about creating a balance and promoting respect for all living creatures.

What does Islam mean to you?

Farah.

I know that this is said all the time, but I really feel that Islam is a way of life, because it encompasses everything: peace, how to live your life, how to live with humanity and with everything around you. It is a very connected religion. I have always admired certain indigenous religions because they connect to everything. Islam is very much like that. It is not limiting. I can live in the West, work for material gain and still be Islamic. I don't have to give all my money to charity. I can practise Islam fully and live in any country I want.

Amber

Islam is a comfort zone for me, a core strength and a foundation. Whenever I have problems or questions, I can turn to the Qur'an for guidance.

For me, Islam has been more of a social experience. I find that the religious aspect of Islam is stressed more in small communities than in large ones. I wish I saw more balance between the social and religious aspects.

Salima

Islam is a practical and spiritual guide to living humanistically. Islam is about developing inner and outer awareness about our spiritual and material lives. Islam can be seen purely as an expression of our faith, and our obligations, and interactions with God and humanity. Islam tells a story and provides real-life examples of how to live and act in justice and peace. At the same time, I see Islam as a civilization of diverse cultures and societies, and intellectual, scientific and other achievements going back 1,400 years. And in this aspect of Islam, we must consider the social, economic, political and cultural developments that occurred within Islamic societies.

The Just

We often hear people say, "Don't question your faith." But without questions, how can we come to a deeper understanding of our faith, our traditions, our history and God? Here we explored questions and concerns we have about Islam.

Farah

I have wondered about homosexuality. I don't know Arabic, so I have to accept what other interpreters tell me (I have always heard that it is against our religion). Once I heard someone speak about homosexuality and that one sentence in the Qur'an could be interpreted so many different ways.

Munira

I find it very hard to understand why there are so many people suffering. I find that hard to reconcile with my beliefs; the common explanation is that God gives you what you deserve.

Maha

I have never worshipped at any one mosque, nor have I cared to. The whole purpose of going to a mosque is to facilitate your encounter with the divine, and if that's not happening, there is no point in going. You might as well pray at home where you can feel the divine presence. I was raised to be wary of anything that threatened my ability to think for myself or to make independent decisions. And the two mosques that I have been to, did not encourage thinking for yourself. They have nothing to do with what Islam actually is, in my view.

There are so many Muslims in Toronto who are living under the poverty line. I don't see mosques doing anything about that. I am a firm believer in God helping those who help themselves. Mosques could be used in much more creative and productive ways than they are. To the extent that they refuse to do so, they are not Islamic. That's something that bothers me.

Zaynab

In the beliefs that I follow, Shia women are supposed to be covered, except for the face and hands, when praying. The logic being that you do not want to distract the men who are praying in the room. But when I am by myself in my home performing my prayers, why do I still need to cover fully? I understand the concept of the "unseen," but does the "unseen" play a role if I am taking a shower as well? Sometimes, honestly, I do not feel like covering myself up completely in my own home. I just want to pray. I have many questions, since there are so many interpretations. And I will continue to question the root of my practices because I believe that to be my Islamic duty. Pursuit of knowledge is an obligation upon every Muslim, as the Prophet has said (pbuh).

Salima

My question is a more historical one about how Islam began. Its inception was a message to address injustice and inequities, but I wonder to what degree it was able to actually transform everyday life, especially for those who were disenfranchised. This a matter for more research but it is something that occupies my mind because Islam in theory I think, and in practice are different. Islam in practice comes alive through people's interpretations, which inform their actions, not to mention other aspects of our societies that shape who we are. For me this is an anthropological quest, one which will help inform my understanding of Islam and how it can be used for change.

Nazneen

I always have questions when I read translations of the Qur'an. For example, they say that when you go to heaven, there will be hur (female angels) for you, and I think to myself: hur for the men, but what about for the women? Makes me wonder because I know that God is fair. That doesn't make sense to me.

Another question I have is that if God is said to be rahman and rahim (beneficent and merciful), then why do people say that if we do wrong we will go to hell? That seems like a contradiction. God is beneficent and merciful, so that when we do wrong, He helps us learn from our mistakes and make better choices. But if God is going to send us to hell anyway, why would he need to be rahman and rahim?

The Just

How does Islam inform social justice?

We shared with one another the various ways Islam has influenced our notions of justice and equity.

Protest in Islamabad, Pakistan for women's right – November 1998

Islam on the Environment

"When one plants a tree, the fruits of which all creatures enjoy, let it be written as charity."

(Prophet Muhammad AI-Hadis)

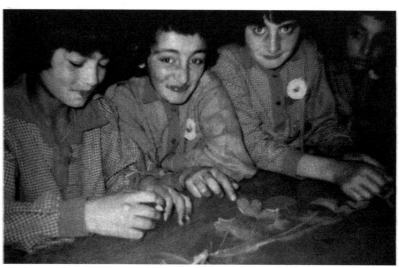

Girls science class Sherkila School
Northern Pakistan – June 1995

Munira

When I was in Lebanon I met a sister who put me in touch with a scholar who had collected references about the environment from the Qur'an.

Do you know how much pollution Muslims contribute to? There are so many things that we are doing that are against our religion. We don't care for the environment. But Islam says we shouldn't, for example, be littering. I think that we should be more proud of the way Islam guides us in regards to the environment. For example, it is haram (a sin) to throw anything on the ground that doesn't belong there. Therefore litter doesn't exist in Islam. Why is it that if we go to Lebanon or Pakistan or for hajj (pilgrimage) and find litter? We know it's haram to eat pork, so we follow that, yet we pollute all the time, but that's not talked about. In so many Muslim countries I saw people throwing things on the ground and nothing happens to them. But if I was sitting there with a piece of bacon, people would jump on me. It's the same thing, in fact it's equivalent.

Islam on Women's Rights

Whoever works righteousness, man or woman, and has Faith, verily, to him will We give a new Life, a life that is good and pure and We will bestow on such their reward according to the best of their actions.

(16.97)

All girls school Karimabad, Hunza
Northern Pakistan – July 1995

Zaynab

There are a lot more rights for women in Islam. The problem is that most women are not aware of them. The right to vote, to own property, to divorce, to education are all prescribed. These are rights that are denied to women because of the patriarchal interpretations. Islam saw the need to address women's oppression and we have done little to implement the message to protect women's rights.

Islam on Humanitarian Service

"And wealth is for the poor refugees who have been forced to flee their homes, forsaking everything, seeking sustenance only from Allah. The wealth is also for those who remained in their city and embraced the faith before them and welcomed those who came to them seeking refuge, who do not begrudge them for what they have been given, but value them above themselves. Those who are able to save themselves from avarice shall certainly prevail."

(59:8-9)

Farah

My role model is my imam (the Aga Khan IV, spiritual leader of the Ismailis). I think that everything that he has done has been incredible. He is recognized all over the world as a great philanthropist. He has created institutions to assist people regardless of their faith, though he focuses in most cases on assisting Muslims. But these institutions don't preach Islam. Our community encourages volunteerism. Each person is reminded of her social, economic, cultural and educational responsibilities as a Muslim; she must dedicate her time and resources to uplift the disenfranchised. The notion of service to one's community is a very important aspect of Islam.

Islam on Social Responsibility
The Almighty Allah judges you neither by your countenance nor your wealth, but by the purity of your hearts and your deeds

The Prophet Muhammad, as reported by Abu Hurairah

Salima

Islam has taught me that my life is not my own, it is intimately connected to humanity; any decision I make, big or small, has a rippling effect, touching those around me and perhaps even those I don't know. Islam teaches social responsibility, and that you are accountable to those around you. In fact it goes so far as looking at systems and structures, whether educational or economic, and asking that each person and each community try to build harmonious societies, in which overconsumption and greed have no place. There is much to learn from this, I believe.

Islam on speaking against Injustice
"Believers, when you are told to make room in assemblies, make room; in return Allah will make room for you in the hereafter. And when you are told to rise (for a good deed), rise up. Allah will exalt those who are truly faithful and have been endowed with knowledge, for Allah is observant of all that you do."

(58:11)

The Just

Maha

Islam is a potentially transformative faith. I think that we are blessed with a beautiful faith. One of the obligations of a Muslim is that if you see injustice you should do something about it. And there is no lack of theoretical justification behind it. If I were in a position to help someone, even on a daily basis, I can't see myself not helping. There is a really beautiful Hadith (saying of the Prophet), "If the last hour strikes and finds you carrying a sapling to the grove to plant go ahead and plant it." I think this is profound.

Beware of the pleas of the oppressed, because they will ask for justice from Allah, and Allah does not deny the rights of the deserving.

The prophet Mohamed, as reported by Ali bin Abi Talib, Al-Hadis

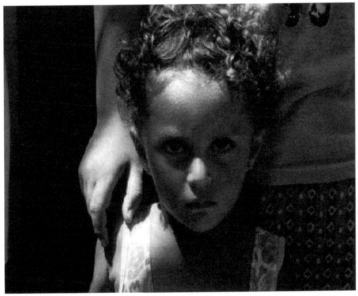

Shaai'ti Refugee Camp, Palestine

Salwa

Islam talks of bearing justice, which it equates to bearing witness to the truth and having the courage to speak out against oppression. My first journey to Palestine allowed me this opportunity to work in the cause of Allah (swt). Standing up for truth is an important mission, if not a responsibility, for Muslims. Our moral responsibilities include kindness, mercy, consideration, respect and a peace-loving outlook for those we come in contact with on a daily basis. We are called upon as Muslims to live up to these moral responsibilities and to continuously improve ourselves so as to strengthen our relationships to one another, and more importantly to Allah (swt).

The Muslim woman activist of today. How is she active?

Salwa

I remember vividly the words of the Ethiopian Israeli officer who interrogated me at the airport. She pulled me aside and questioned me tirelessly and tediously. After this interrogation and her feeble attempt at breaking me down, these were her parting words as she handed me my passport and papers: "You are brave for travelling alone." I remember how ironic and mocking these words were. I walked out and realized that I was not brave for coming to be with my brothers and sisters. The brave ones are the Palestinians who live in the refugee camps. The ones who live under curfew, suffer from lack of education or from high unemployment and poverty; the brave ones have their homes confiscated or demolished during the night, endure the daily terror of Israeli settlers who harass and violently attack them. Those are the brave ones; this is the message I want to send out. These people are awe-inspiring. They have shown resilience and unshakeable steadfastness. These are the people we should be supporting, standing up for, and showing solidarity with.

I came away with an increased sense of perseverance and strength. I came away realizing that I had more to do, not only as a Muslim or as a Palestinian, but also as a human being. I believe this is a call to all decent and humane individuals; it is a call to the human conscience. We must continue to raise awareness for all struggles, the Palestinian struggle or the Iraqi struggle, and speak out against oppression and illegal occupation and human rights abuses. We must continue to struggle and fight for these causes as part of our moral responsibility.

The Just

Mezghan

I think I am an activist in almost everything I do. I try to represent Islam as a Muslim woman and in particular an Afghan Ismaili Muslim woman.

When I am at home, I always try, usually indirectly, to help my family deal with their problems using my knowledge of Islam. I show them through my actions. I try to be a role model, representing an Afghan Ismaili Muslim woman within the framework of her culture, religion and ethics.

At school, I try to be a role model for other students and to educate them about Islam and about Muslim women. I am enthusiastic about representing my culture, my religion and my country.

Amber

I consider my writing to be a form of activism. I choose to write about various aspects of Islam, and am thus able to convey a slice of life not usually accessible to the "majority" of Canadian readers. And I'm very lucky and proud to be a part of this book. I may not be marching in the streets or founding an organization, but I do my bit!

Salima

My activism is in the political, social and spiritual realms. I have committed my life to various causes: women's issues, cultural and faith concerns, development issues, youth and anti-racism. These are areas where I want to work with Muslims and non-Muslims alike, to respond to inequities within government, educational institutions, faith-based communities, and families and homes. I want to continue to build creative, positive and progressive spaces for diverse Muslims. My activism is deeply connected to the Ismaili community, but my commitment has expanded over the past ten years to the ummah in general and to other marginalized groups within Canada and abroad. I pray that I can continue my work throughout my life.

The reality of Allah is boundless

Majlis al-Mughnî
The Enricher

And hold fast, all together, by the rope which Allah (stretches out for you), and be not divided among yourselves; and remember with gratitude Allah's favour on you; for ye were enemies and He joined your hearts in love, so that by His Grace, ye became brethren; and ye were on the brink of the pit of Fire, and He saved you from it. Thus doth Allah make His Signs clear to you: That ye may be guided.

(3.103)

One of the challenges of representation is the question of who is represented. Who speaks for Islam and its various communities? The persecution of marginalized Muslim groups by dominant groups has created rifts, fear, alienation, and even sectarian violence among Muslims. The Muslim voices primarily heard in the mainstream represent dominant, powerful groups and individuals who do not reflect the diversity of Islam.

What Sunnis know about Shias or Shias know about Ahmadis or Ahmadis know about Ismailis is as much a historical problem of falsified, biased accounts, and destruction of cultures and traditions as it is a problem of present-day slander via the internet, books, political speeches or religious sermons. Thus, the problem appears to lie in miscommunication and misinformation. Our representations of Islam may not be fair or just to all Muslims and of course no one person or group can represent all Muslims, but through communication and knowledge we can begin to challenge the discrediting and alienation of other Muslims.

We don't know each other as Muslims. We don't know one another's histories, struggles, and traditions. In order to reclaim our right to represent ourselves in the fairest way possible, we need to learn about one another.

We discussed our feelings about the various interpretations of Islam and why we have been kept from knowing one another. As well, we talked about how to challenge this lack of knowing. We have begun a process of breaking down barriers that many Muslims are still working hard to preserve. We will achieve little as an ummah with such discrimination and hatred. To move forward, we have tried to learn from one another and to support one another in our struggles.

The Enricher

In order to confront the myths we have about each other, we attempt to expose what we actually think about one another as Muslims.

What do you think about the various interpretations of Islam?

Zaynab (Shia Ithnashari)

If the Qur'an were clear-cut there would not be so many sects. You can't understand the sects without looking at history and finding out why they exist. In my personal journey, I have done this. The essence within the sects is the same. We have branched out in different ways. I think the killings and wars that happen because of these differences are stupid. Sometimes I think that they are just the result of testosterone.

Farah (Shia Ismaili)

I don't spend too much time thinking about the other sects. The only time they become an issue is when I am told that I am not a Muslim, when I feel threatened by other Muslims. I do not wish to judge others or criticize other sects. You practise the way you are most comfortable and I will do the same. I just wish we could see beyond the lines of difference, and then we would be a stronger and more united group who could fight back against the distortion of our religion.

Maha (Sunni)

I think the many interpretations of Islam are a great thing. There is so much that we could potentially learn from one another. The first time I went to an Ithnashari masjid was cool because I saw things I had never seen before, things that I found really beautiful. There was a room where they kept the tesias. (A tesia is a reproduction of the shrine of Imam Hussein, grandson of the Prophet (pbuh) and martyred third Imam of the Shias.) Tesias are made of gold, crystal or paper and are beautiful. This is something I wouldn't have been exposed to had I not come to this masjid. I went during the first days of Muharram (the month of mourning commemorating the death of Imam Hussein) and I had never seen people do matam (act of grieving) before. It was at the Jaffry centre and the women's section is behind the men's. The elderly women were beating themselves quite vigorously and calling out,

"Hussein! Hussein! Hussein!" I found it amazing that people could work themselves into such a fever of emotion and then come down from it. Such exposure to different sects broadens your horizons. It's a shame that there is sectarian violence in Pakistan, people going to mosques and gunning each other down. That's appalling.

Salima (Shia Ismaili)

The fact that there are differing interpretations within a religion is an indication of the various ways religion comes alive through people. I think that plurality of any kind is a beautiful thing. To me, this is a sign of Allah's limitlessness. If God cannot be encapsulated in one way, how can we chain ourselves to our beliefs so tightly that we cannot accept different ways of understanding? I say, power to the Sunnis, Ahmadis, Shia Ithnasharis, Ismailis and any other groups for living their Islam, as long as it is not imposed on others.

Munira (Shia Ithnashari)

I think we practise the way we do because of what we believe. It's hard to communicate or interact with those who don't believe what you do, especially when they are also Muslim. I don't know about every other sect but it is still my responsibility to educate people. And everyone is answerable for their actions. Sisters from other sects ask, "How can you do this? Does that make sense to you?" and we debate. I think that we need to be understanding. But it's hard. A lot of people will insist that their way is the better way. I have to admit that I do believe the way I practise is the better way. People believe in a religion when they are convinced that it is the best way, at least they should be if they chose to practise in that manner.

Salwa (Sunni)

Sunnis constitute ninety percent of the entire Muslim community. But I know that belonging to the majority sect does not give me the right to walk around acting mightier than members of the other sects. I believe that most Sunnis, especially the ones I know in our generation, feel the same way. The political and theological differences that have divided us into different sects have isolated us to the point that we have no dialogue with one another. This is not right. I believe that we should promote dialogue among different sects. I have many opportunities to enjoy healthy conversations with my Shia friends. It's all about having enough respect for one another to be able to sit down and discuss our differences and the similarities that bond us together in the brotherhood and sisterhood of Islam.

Mezghan (Shia Ismaili)

The existence of many different sects or interpretations of Islam does not surprise me. I think of it as a natural part of every religion. If you look at Christianity, for example, you will find many different sects as well.

We also discussed how we felt about learning from one another and the different interpretations and sects we represent

Nazneen (Sunni)

This was a very good opportunity for me to be with people from different sects. I have never had a chance to meet such people, get to know them and to listen to their views. By talking to all these women, I realized that we Sunni Muslims have caused such rifts among ourselves, that it is not surprising we don't have much tolerance for non-Muslims. After our sessions, I felt ashamed that we (Sunnis) have been so intolerant. I don't remember if I have intentionally or unintentionally said anything hurtful to anyone, because when you have power sometimes it's hard to see its consequences. Our sessions made me aware that Sunnis have power and it affects other people's lives.

And as the dominant group that often oppresses other Muslims, we are responsible for how other Muslims feel about themselves or others. I have also come to realize by meeting others how much we have in common. How the basics are the same. From this experience I have learned not to take the privileges of being a Sunni for granted. I will now be very careful with my actions and words and will help to educate other Sunnis as well. We talk about unity in Islam, but unity does not come from holding hands or praying five times daily, unity comes from tolerance and respect for others.

Munira (Shia Ithnashari)

Learning from all the women was very interesting but not without the stress due to our "differences."

Salwa (Sunni)

I believe this is a fabulous opportunity to meet and to exchange personal narratives with one another. Every woman in this group has strong, unwavering religious convictions and attractive personalities that make the sharing process enjoyable and enriching. I feel that these kinds of dialogue sessions help to break down the walls between us and to build the foundation that will pave the way for progress.

Farah (Shia Ismaili)

I enjoyed meeting some intelligent and interesting women. This was challenging, because I was angry in certain situations when I felt as though people were judging others and not being as open-minded as we had promised to be at the first session. I thought that this was supposed to be a safe space but often it was not. It's one thing to express one's views, but it's quite another to express it as the correct or only view.

Maha (Sunni)

I enjoyed meeting all the women. Hearing the different viewpoints was really valuable. I have come together with Muslim women before, but by chance; this was my first experience of a concerted attempt to tell where each of us is coming from.

At times I heard views that are not sanctioned by my interpretation of the faith. But I respect the fact that everyone can come up with her own interpretation of the faith, as long as I don't feel it is imposed on me. When one woman stated strong opinions about the veil and modesty, I noticed some people in the group had a problem with that. But I wasn't bothered because I didn't take it seriously.

Mezghan (Shia Ismaili)

I think our differences make us unique and give us an opportunity to learn from each other, absorb positive attitudes, and adopt what we lack or admire.

The Enricher

Zaynab (Shia Ithnashari)

This was amazing because my first encounter with Sunnis was very negative. As a Shia Ithnashari I believe in muta (temporary marriages). I was virtually labeled a prostitute when walking into a Sunni mosque, by both men and women. In this group, meeting women who are educated and who have different opinions and open minds, I have a better view of things. It helps me look at us as a whole again.

Salima (Shia Ismaili)

Collaborative dialogue among women who normally don't have the chance to talk to one another is exciting. This has been a dream come true because we are the ummah of the future and we are taking steps towards a more unified future through our efforts and hard work.

There are things that are keeping us apart, keeping us from "knowing" each other. How can we unpack these?

Nazneen (Sunni)

Right now, the only barrier I see is that we accept what we are told without question. People don't know about other Muslims' religious practices and the information they are given is distorted. The leaders are the ones who often pass on distorted information. But people accept whatever they hear from these leaders, even though Islam itself tells us to think and accept anything only if our hearts and minds believe it.

Salima (Shia Ismaili)

It is difficult to access knowledge about one another that is not written for inflammatory or discrediting purposes and so we continue to live in ignorance. I have heard ridiculous stories about minority Muslim groups. We need to provide information that steers the masses away from the kafir ideology, the belief that some Muslims are not Muslim at all but are unbelievers. I would leave it to God to judge.

Historically there has been division among us. This was due to political differences or different interpretation of Islam. Today, however, I believe that the leaders-mullahs, imams and others-help maintain their power and superiority by propagating one "true" version of Islam to keep the masses agreeable and encourage oppression against minority Muslim groups. If someone says that it is divinely ordained that "this" is Islam and "that" is not, then he can justify decisions and actions that hurt those who do not fall within these boundaries.

Zaynab (Shia Ithnashari)

I think that it comes from culture, from history, from ignorance. It comes from not being able to get to know people. I met Shia sisters through a fluke. I didn't know anyone who was Shia. I was corresponding with someone in the UK who e-mailed someone in Michigan who e-mailed Munira. Then there was a get-together of sisters in Toronto and I went to it and that was that. But for a convert who knows nobody, it is very difficult. If it is difficult to find people of my own sect, how much harder would it be to find people of another sect?

Mezghan (Shia Ismaili)

One major factor that keeps us from knowing each other is the desire that everyone be like us. We try to change people. We forget that we cannot change people until they themselves want to change. In this struggle to correct other people-to change them-and to make them the way we are, we will not only fail but we will also damage our existing relationships.

Munira (Shia Ithnashari)

Two things: we are busy and we live in a society in which the majority are not Muslims. When we do have free time and want to grow and expand, we learn from our own people, about our own people, our own sect. This depends on the level of faith you decide to live by. If I spend the majority of my time with non-Muslims, chances are that I will not learn a lot about my religion. I try as much as possible to be with people who will help increase my knowledge and devotion to Islam. I spend a lot of time with people who share the same beliefs as I do.

If you are spending time with other people, they think you are out to convert them. This creates a lot of pressure. If you and I are good friends, how can we relate if we're not the same? I had a friend of mine at university who was Christian but was not sure what she wanted to be at that time. So I introduced her to Islam and brought her to a few events; but we are so culturally driven that I think it scared her. Now she is a born-again Christian, and our relationship is very difficult.

Maha (Sunni)

People shouldn't fear difference. The opposition that you find among Muslims is totally based on fear of the unknown.

What are some of the things we can do to bring down the barriers we face?

Mezghan (Shia Ismaili)

We should spend less time focusing on how different others are and criticizing how they should practise Islam, instead we should try to accept them as they are.
We should educate ourselves about other sects so that we can understand them. We should educate others by spreading awareness. Communicating and interacting diminishes the distance between us.

Nazneen (Sunni)

Everyone participating in this project is a member of a family, a community, so she should pass on what she has learned here. Word of mouth goes far, and with new information there is opportunity for people to change. I shared my personal experiences so others could learn from them. If we behave in ignorance (as we have done in this group at certain times) we will never get anywhere.

Farah (Shia Ismaili)

First of all, we need to recognize that there will be conflict when working with "different" Muslim women. When I came to this group, I envisioned a happy bonding session. But it didn't turn out that way. That kind of interaction will not happen overnight. It will be a difficult process. We are discussing deeply held beliefs. And, comments can be hurtful. I also think change has to happen on an individual basis. Everyone has to make a conscious effort to be open-minded. I may not be able to speak at a mosque, but forums such as these are great and are steps in the right direction, even if there are only a handful of us.

Salwa (Sunni)

I believe that our generation, and the ones after it, will effect positive change and begin to break down the barriers between us. We need to talk to one another and listen to one another with respect and tolerance. I have many Muslim friends, but one of my dearest friends is a Christian Arab. Our relationship is a reciprocal interaction of love, respect and tolerance. If I am able to build this relationship, then surely we as Muslims can put our efforts together to build relationships based on our faith's moral obligations. We only need to look at the life of the Prophet Muhammad (sallallaahu alayhe wasallam), how he interacted with his followers with so much love and tolerance, and use this as a model for our interactions with one another.

Salima (Shia Ismaili)

This project and book is an obvious step for me.

Munira (Shia Ithnashari)

It would be nice for us to come together or even for community leaders to come together. I mentioned a group, Sura, that will come together, that will gather community leaders from different sects once a month to discuss issues, such as school curriculum that affect the entire community. I used to think, before I came to Islam, that there was one Islam, one people. But I learned that we have sects. I learned a lot from our group discussions about what Ismailis face or Sunnis think. To increase our knowledge is great. But more importantly, our leaders, who set examples for our communities, should be getting together on a regular basis and showing a united front on common issues.

The Enricher

Maha (Sunni)

We need to have a humanistic interpretation of our faith that accepts different interpretations of Islam and doesn't see some as less Muslim than others. Fundamental psychological changes need to take place, people need to change what they think and how they feel. I don't see how one can move forward without them.

Zaynab (Shia Ithnashari)

People should start having more open minds. If you choose not to see anything else, you will see only black and white.

A lot of Muslims who I've encountered have been very narrow minded. They are kind and gentle people, but they are not open minded. That's the reality that I am dealing with. Am I compromising myself by being with Muslims who are closed minded? These are the questions that run through my mind.

Final thoughts.

In this chapter we discussed how fear and lack of knowledge keeps us from knowing each other. What are those fears based on? And why this ignorance? Different interpretations, which are due to diverse histories, traditions, and practices, perhaps bring out feelings of insecurity and the need to protect or legitimize a particular version of the faith. We see this not only in Islam. The West has achieved its supremacy by devaluing other cultures or belief systems. This is not what Islam asks for. Living in harmony with our plurality is an Islamic vision, one that we should celebrate and work towards.

To thee We sent the Scripture in truth, confirming the scripture that came before it, and guarding it in safety: so judge between them by what Allah hath revealed, and follow not their vain desires, diverging from the Truth that hath come to thee. To each among you have we prescribed a law and an open way. If Allah had so willed, He would have made you a single people, but (His plan is) to test you in what He hath given you: so strive as in a race in all virtues. The goal of you all is to Allah; it is He that will show you the truth of the matters in which ye dispute;

(5.48)

Women and men we are but from the same truth.

Majlis al-Muqsit

The Equitable

Women's participation and leadership, in the development, decision-making and interactions of their communities are paramount for ideological, as well as social, economic and political enhancement and change. The process of women coming together to talk about issues impacting them within their communities can lead to empowerment as well as analyses of and challenges to the barriers of participation.

Of course, specific cultural, social, economic, religious and political factors must be taken into consideration in this kind of work. In this project, the women have taken direct steps to engage in a collective process of dialogue about our cultural and religious communities. We have discussed what we see as the challenges within the communities and the possibilities for change.

In speaking about our communities, we decided to talk about the divide, confluence and interaction between culture and religion, because in many cases they are so closely tied together. Often, culture is framed within a religious discourse of gender domination and subjugation. Islam, in theory, is to be adapted by each culture without intruding into that culture, but rather enhancing it and in many cases offering a humanitarian perspective. What follows are explorations of the intimate, at times convoluted, relationship between culture and religion.

The Believers, men and women, are protectors of one another: they enjoin what is just, and forbid what is evil: they observe regular prayers, practise regular charity, and obey Allah and His Messenger. On them will Allah pour His mercy: for Allah is Exalted in power, Wise.

(9:71)

The Equitable

Defining religion.

Amber

Religion is like a sibling to me. I don't remember when we met, we don't always agree, but I love it fiercely and I can't imagine my life without it. It isn't a "practice" you try once in a while, it's a way of life and I'm still trying to find my way.

Zaynab

I do not like the word "religion" because there is no set definition. Overall, this is how I would define religion: belief in and reverence for a supernatural power or powers regarded as creator and governor of the universe; personal or institutionalized system grounded in such belief and worship; the life or condition of a person in a religious order; a set of beliefs, values, and practices based on the teachings of a spiritual leader.

I think the best definition I have come across is Susan Law: "A religion is the organized set of beliefs that encode a person's or group's attitudes toward, and understanding of, the essence or nature of reality."

Salima

Religion provides us with the possibility of exploring the inner and outer meaning of life. It's an avenue through which to explore the divine. It is a sense of belonging to a group who have shared values and forms of religious communication.

Salwa

Religion is my moral compass. Religion is how I live my life everyday, according to the beliefs, moral and ritual obligations, and basic tenets of Islam. Religion is my faith and commitment to the omnipotent, omniscient and almighty Creator.

Mezghan

To me religion is like a boat that saves one from sinking. It is also a means of uniting people to care for each other and to help each other.

Defining culture.

Zaynab

Culture is something that is acquired, a human pattern that I believe is always changing, it's what makes groups of people distinct from others in the way they think, live, eat, behave, their interests, their characters.

Amber

Culture is everything. It is the way I dress, the way I speak, the way I relate (or don't relate) to other people. I've become this way because of the community in which I grew up, through social experiences or communicated symbols and traditions.

Salwa

Culture is the customs, food, music, dance, literature and art shared by the community to which I belong. These are what identify me as belonging to a certain group of individuals, without respect to religion. The Arabs, for example, share a common culture but have disparate religious affiliations.

Mezghan

I think culture is a means of expression. It is a way of expressing or representing your beliefs, values and norms. It reflects your open mindedness and pride for your identity.

Salima

Culture is an evolving way of living. It defines social interactions. It provides the basis for religious, political, economic and social expressions and development.

Culture and religion: their interconnection and intersection.

Zaynab

"Go and seek knowledge," the Prophet said. But people don't. They are content with their environment, and their mentality, questioning nothing. It bothers me when women are like this, regardless of their religion or culture. Some women question things but won't say anything because they are afraid to speak out. I think that women in this society should be questioning many things. In terms of culture, the more you seek, the more you learn. The whole philosophy behind the Qur'an is that everything is logical. I think that ninety percent of Muslims would describe things in their culture as Islamic, when they have nothing to do with Islam. For example, covering the face or walking behind the man. Where in Islam does it say to do these things? It's the ummah that perpetuates this. My partner says that there is a difference between Muslims and Islam. He himself is an Arab and Shia. He says, "Always go with what Islam teaches and not what people say. You have to learn and seek the knowledge for yourself."

Nazneen

In my mind there are only two times when culture and religion clearly intersect: when we are born and when we die. These are times when the essence of Islam and culture can both be seen. Besides that, we have changed many things and intertwined them so much that we can't differentiate any more between Islam and culture.

Salwa

Culture and religion are two clearly distinct things for me. Growing up in a typical Arab family, I became very frustrated because it took me time and knowledge to identify that there was a difference between something being Islamic and something being Arabic. I make a conscious effort not to confuse the two, even today. However the way that religion has complemented our cultures is very interesting. But we must never lose the distinction between religion and culture, as the other women here have highlighted, especially when it comes to social and political practices masquerading as Islam.

Musayaf Ismaili Castle, Musayaf, Syria

Mezghan

Culture and religion usually go side by side. For example, in Afghanistan we did not really feel that we practised Islam because it was just part of our life and the way we lived. However, sometimes when culture and religion interfere with each other, then we should probably practise Islam according to the culture we are living in. For example, while living in the West, it is difficult to pray five times a day.

Munira

There are Islamic requirements that override culture. My interpretation of Islam says that you should wear loose-fitting clothes, cover your hair, neck and body except for your face and hands. So, if I go to Pakistan and see women wearing sheer scarves over their heads and their arms are not completely covered, I see that as cultural and not religious. In my opinion, culture is fine as long as it does not contradict religious prescriptions. Women must educate themselves regarding Islamic laws because they may find themselves in a culture that denies these rights. For example, women in Afghanistan who are forced to wear a full-body veil and are not allowed to work. If women are educated about their Islamic rights they can have a different view and rise up against culture. When my husband and I were introduced, we discussed many important issues before deciding to get married. Islam insists that you know the person you are marrying. However, when my uncle got married he met his wife on his wedding day and had never exchanged a word with her, directly or indirectly, prior to that day. That is culture. Our Islamic rights exist for a reason and we must be aware of them.

Salima

I agree with those who talked about some of the problems with cultural practices that oppress or subjugate under the guise of religion. I want to discuss the importance of cultures in the expression of religious ideas. Islamic architecture is a great example of how Islamic concepts are used in the design of physical structures. If you examine mosques or castles or forts in countries where Islam flourished, you will see that the design of these

The Equitable

structures reflect local culture, even though they share the underlying theme of expressing God's unity and limitlessness. So for instance, in Turkey, you see the use of floral design a great deal more than in Syria or Spain, where geometrical design is dominant. Even the use of colour is peculiar to the local context. I think this is beautiful. It says so much about how we convey religious ideas differently and uniquely. One of the things that Muslims were very conscious of as Islam spread is how Islam could be integrated with the local cultural milieu and this shaped how Islam showed up in various ways throughout the world and continues to do so.

Jalaludin Rumi's Tomb Konya, Turkey

Farah

I think it's harder for me to talk about the distinction between culture and religion because of the way I live my Islam. I think it's easy to do if you look at other places. If I look at Afghanistan, for example, I can clearly distinguish what is cultural and what is Islamic. Look at all the drug trafficking that has been going on. You can't tell me this is Islamic, because that is completely contradictory. The West is patriarchal; does that mean Christianity is patriarchal? Not necessarily. Ireland is violent. Does that mean Christianity is violent? Not necessarily. There needs to be a clear distinction made between what is religious and what is cultural. But, the fact is people who are in charge have sexist attitudes and children are socialized to be the same way. And I don't know how it will change because it is internalized. So much undoing is required.

Maha

Culture and Islam intersect in ways that are both negative and positive. When societies that have cultural practices such as spousal abuse, denying education to girls, or keeping women in their homes, you will find that these practices pre-date the arrival of Islam. In villages in India, Hindu women face the same constraints as Muslim women. In this case, cultural practices are masquerading as Islamic.

But I have a problem with dividing religion and culture so sharply all the time. For example, in Egypt, infertile women visit the shrine of religious saints as a form of therapy. But because shrine worship is considered shirk (heretical), because you are assigning divine power to something other than God, these women are condemned. But the women believe they are carrying out a religiously mandated practice and that it is helping them. They feel that it is bringing them closer to God, because in their minds there is a distinction between praying to God and praying to someone who is pious and who might intercede on their behalf because of his close proximity to God. I don't see what's accomplished by condemning practices like this as cultural and not Islamic. Yes, it is cultural, but Islam has been absorbed into this culture in a way that is beneficial for all involved. So, why does it have to be condemned?

The cultural and religious communities that Muslims create or are a part of are not generally speaking very different from other marginalized communities in Canada. We face many similar economic and social challenges. Perhaps we can frame the challenges that we see within our communities within this complex relationship of culture and religion in order to meet the needs of the members of our communities.

Maha

One of the primary challenges our communities face is the belief that we are unable to think for ourselves. There is a real sense among us that we are not able to produce religious knowledge that can be taken seriously. If only people were confident in their ability to think on their own. I think that is the basis for everything else.

There are power dynamics within our Sunni communities that contribute to this resistance to thinking independently. It seems that many sheiks or imams benefit from our not thinking for ourselves. It reinforces their power.

If people understood that this is about power and domination, it would help us to create more humanistic interpretations of the faith. There is no reason why these leaders should have a monopoly over knowledge.

Our history has been obscured, in particular the early history of our faith, when it was a flexible and dynamic religion. This knowledge is not getting out there. It is all very well for scholars such as Fatima Mernissi and Laila Ahmed to be out there, but they are not reaching the audience that needs to be reached. The fact is that most women in the Muslim world are

The Equitable

not going to respond to feminist theory or the Western perception of human rights. If you can make the argument for the elevation of equal status in an Islamic idiom and couch it in Islamic language, that is something they might accept. And it may actually go towards influencing women's lives on a daily basis.

Farah

I think that we as an Ismaili community have advanced by leaps and bounds. We have programs in place for abused children, abused elders, and abused women. And it has taken a long time to get here. Leaders and even the community on some level have not wanted to acknowledge these problems But that is changing. It is challenging and changing both thinking and attitudes.

Zaynab

You can take a textbook home and learn the theory but you can't put it into practice unless you have someone to guide you. My current partner helps me, but because I don't belong to one particular community I have to seek everything out myself. As a result, I have many questions that can't be answered.

As a woman of colour I face discrimination. Within Muslim communities there is discrimination among people who are not ethnically the same. Some converts look Mediterranean or European and are "passable" but others are not. I stay within the Shia community by sticking with those friends whom I initially met. But I think that this racism needs to be addressed and eradicated.

Salima

I think that as Ismailis we have many privileges, because of the nature and structure of our community. We have a strong leader who keeps us together and guides us both spiritually and materially. But I don't think we always hear everything. The issue of classism comes to mind. We don't acknowledge poverty within our community in Canada and we have an image of being an affluent community. The Imam says, "The accumulation of wealth is not bad, it is greed and overconsumption that are problematic. Produce to assist not only yourselves but also your community." That is a wonderful principle and ethic to live by, but I think it translates within our community as classism.

On a more general level within the ummah I see a huge problem with the limitations placed on critical thinking. This is something I have felt in many of my discussions with other Muslims. There are certain things one is not allowed to question. Often, we examine our history through glorification. While there is much to celebrate, the fact is Islam flourished through human beings and as great as they may have been, if we cannot examine their histories critically, then we are promoting a fantasy. I am not suggesting this to discredit anyone but rather to have a richer and more real understanding of Islamic civilization and history. Why is questioning equated with blasphemy?

Munira

Problems with ethnicity are a big concern. If you are from Lebanon, you go to the Lebanese mosque, if you from Pakistan, you go to the Pakistani mosque, if you are from East Africa, you go to the East African mosque, and so on. If you are a convert, you are utterly lost because the service may not be in English and people may treat you badly for being racially or ethnically different. This is our biggest problem. Providing knowledge is another problem. There are not enough scholars to go to the mosques and talk to people. And language has become a problem. We have a new English-speaking generation that does not know their language. So when they go to mosques where only Urdu or Arabic or Persian is being spoken, they don't understand. Many mosques are facing the difficulty of accommodating our elderly people but also making it interesting and accessible to youth. It's very hard.

Nazneen

In our community (Pakistani), I am concerned about the relationship between parents and children. I see that many parents don't have a positive relationship with their children. I believe that parents should be held accountable for this. At times I see that parents expect their kids to be like they were back home, which ends up alienating the kids and at other times parents push their kids to assimilate and be gora (take on Western values). Once this happens, parents become concerned that their children have lost their culture. There is obviously a challenge faced by Pakistani parents in providing balanced parenting. That fosters a healthy balance in values between Pakistani culture, Islam, and the West.

One of the first steps in making changes for women is knowing what their needs are and what specific challenges they face within their communities

Salwa

I do not believe that Muslim women are represented enough in our community. But we have the potential for developing great women leaders in our ummah. We should start joining the many existing organizations, and if that's not possible we should continue creating forums such as these. I believe that women offer different leadership abilities than men. We offer a broader vision and richer creativity for a future that would benefit all of humanity. I think that we should start exercising our equal rights within Islam and open doors for us, rather than waiting for others to open them for us.

Nazneen

Some Muslims cannot picture a woman living alone, single, without a man, not married. I constantly feel the pressure. It doesn't affect me too much, but it is always there. Many women have to deal with this.

Secondly, I see many women from back home who work here but are not given the same kind of freedom they had back home. Their husbands and families say, "We will let you work but you can't have a life outside of work and your family." So their experiences are limited.

Mezghan

Being a Muslim woman living in the West, I face many challenges, such as being questioned about my faith. I am not an expert in Islam. I am in the process of learning. I have my own questions. However, I want to know about the roles and positions of women in other religions in order to understand my religion better. I want to find out if Islam has filled the gaps that existed in the religions that appeared before Islam.

Munira

Right now what is lacking are women-only sessions with scholars. Such sessions do exist but they are not widely accessible. I would prefer women from many different backgrounds participating together. Right now, I attend sessions every Saturday with a group of ethnically diverse young adults, male and female. We talk about various issues in a safe environment. We need similar groups for women only.

Salima

We may be able to include women in our religious institutions, even in visible positions, but these women are sometimes co-opted by sexist and patriarchal institutions. An element that is missing is real ideological change that makes women's perspectives a part of everything we do, including how we practise our faith.

Maha

Women are not taken seriously. It's not as though they don't have power and authority in their lives, but from an orthodox standpoint their contributions to the faith are not recognized. As Muslims they're not taken as seriously as Muslim men. Their desire for religious needs is not nurtured. They are viewed as the auxiliary corps of Muslims. I think that a lot of Muslim women feel cut off from their faith because they don't have access to the same sorts of religious knowledge as men do, to this beautiful, tremendous history, to this body of thought and practice that is Islam. Who knows how many brilliant contributions could have been made by women if they just had access to this knowledge.

Farah

In the Ismaili community, the newly arrived immigrant women jamat from Central Asia have so many things to deal with. For them there are even more barriers than for the rest of us. They are exposed to a totally new culture. They have a language barrier. And they have economic barriers. If they are married, they may have to work such long hours that they do

The Equitable

not see their spouses. And if they have children, they are worried about preserving their culture. And, of course, jamat khana here is different from what they are used to, so they must feel uncomfortable. I think the feelings of exclusion for women in their situations would be really overwhelming. Within our community, these are the women I am concerned about.

Zaynab

I think that time is lacking. It is very rare that I have met young Muslim women who are not married; if they're not married, it's because they are teenagers. Apparently at my age I should be married. It's funny because I never pictured myself being married. But since I've been in the community, I feel more pressure. I think single women have more time then married women. Single women in our age group can organize and make change. Whenever I go to study sessions and we talk about women's issues, the sheik will quote the Qu'ran and make positive statements about women in Islam. But then he will go home and, with his personal, sexist views, treat the women in his life badly. I think people need to realize these contradictions. True change can only happen when we practise what we preach.

Final thought.

To ignore or to fail to address the needs and concerns of half the members of any community is an injustice. As Muslims we are directed to be responsible to one another and to provide for and know one another.

O mankind! We created you from a single (pair) of a male and a female, and made you into nations and tribes, that ye may know each other (not that ye may despise (each other). Verily the most honoured of you in the sight of Allah is (he who is) the most righteous of you. And Allah has full knowledge and is well acquainted (with all things).

(49.13)

Let the pain be healed through love and peace.

Majlis ar-Rahim
The Merciful

A person who overcomes others by physical strength is not powerful; the truly powerful are those who control their wrath when aroused to anger.

The Prophet Muhammad, as reported by Abu Hurairah, Sahih al-Bukhari p962

September 11.

When major global events occur, many of us don't know how to make our voices heard, we feel our perspective will not reach the right people or won't make a difference. Often it is assumed that some groups have nothing to say, nothing of any value to the public anyway. Therefore, in mainstream discourses, the "experts" provide analysis. Following September 11, most of the so-called experts who spoke about Islam, Muslims, and their alleged connection to September 11 were not Muslim. Muslims were kept out of the discussions. They were asked to pick sides: us or them. Who was the "us" and who was the "them"? It was a question few people were asking. What was evident was that Muslims did not have an opportunity to talk about their experiences of September 11, the impact this event had on their lives and their analyses of events.

We use this space to tell our stories and share our reflections about September 11, as Muslim women. This is our time to speak about it.

Nor can a bearer of burdens bear another's burdens if one heavily laden should call another to (bear) his load. Not the least portion of it can be carried (by the other). Even though he be nearly related. Thou canst but admonish such as fear their Lord unseen and establish regular Prayer. And whoever purifies himself does so for the benefit of his own soul; and the destination (of all) is to Allah.

(35:18)

Telling our stories about the events of September 11.

Where were you on September 11?

Zaynab

I remember walking into my workplace. Everyone was listening to the radio. I asked a coworker, what was going on. She said, "The World Trade Centre is falling!" I did not take her seriously because she is always speaking of stocks and the market. Then I started to listen to the radio with the others. I was in complete shock…

I do not think it really hit me until I saw the footage on TV. I was not concerned really about who did it or why, but rather how people were dealing with it and what these poor people must be feeling or experiencing at that moment. It was too shocking.

Salwa

I was at work, sitting at my desk, business as usual, and there was a buzz at the workplace and so I decided to grab my radio and find out what was going on. I remember trying to get an AM station. Finally I got a station and I remember listening, listening and listening

My feelings at that moment were of absolute fear, fear of the unknown, fear of suspicion, fear of more loss of life that might come.

The thoughts going through my mind at the time were about my family and friends. I had to get in touch with them, connect with them. I was on the phone calling everyone that I loved and they were telling me what was going on there for them. I remember sitting at my desk bawling my eyes out, telling everybody that I loved them. I just didn't think this was real. This conversation has taken me back to that time and I haven't really talked about it, so it is very hard for me. (Tears run down her face.)

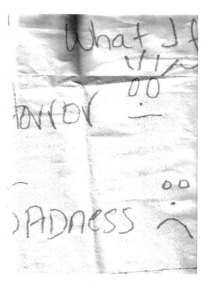

Mezghan

On September 11, we had just arrived from Pakistan. We were living at the reception centre and we watched everything that was happening and it was so horrifying to me. It reminded me of all the loss and destruction that had been happening in Afghanistan.

I thought I was coming here to live in peace, to forget the destruction and killing, but after this it scared me. I felt that everywhere we go, violence will follow us. It was very hard for me.

I was very sad about the lives that were taken.

I was thinking about what was going to happen to Muslims. We were afraid of what would happen to Muslims in Canada and the United States, and we were hearing about Muslim women with the hijab who had been attacked on the streets. I was scared. I felt insecure.

Amber

At the news station, in one newsroom we had feeds coming in from all over the world and they were showing the twin towers on fire and then they immediately showed that footage from Palestine where people were cheering, which was then proven to have been false.

These were some of the most horrific things I had ever seen. I was scared but had to continue doing my job. At the time it did not even cross my mind that Muslims were involved, but within the hour, they started talking about Islamic terrorists and I became very upset. It felt like the beginning of something apocalyptic, and here we are two years later.

The question of why this happened did not come up in the newsroom. They were not concerned with that. A week later they wanted to understand the causes and they started to talk about jihad. They were planning to do a piece that described it (the event) as basically Muslims wanting to convert by the sword. I went up to the anchor and told him that jihad was actually about an internal struggle. Then he changed the story and made it about the internal struggle.

Hearing about all those people who lost their lives reminded me of the people in my country who were being killed each day.

The Merciful

Farah

My reaction: please, please don't let this be the work of a Muslim. I sat in front of the television for about twelve hours. I did not eat or move. I felt dread because all the "evidence" was pointing to Islamic fundamentalists. I felt fear. What would this do to all of us, to the Muslims who had made so much progress? How much backlash would we face? Then I felt sadness. I cried for all the people on the planes and their families, for all the people in the Trade Center and their families. I cried for all the police and fire fighters and their families. I cried for the way the world was going to change. I was horrified that anybody could commit such a crime against humanity.

Nazneen

I was at work and honestly I did not know anything about the World Trade Center and that it was a symbol of pride for America. A woman came to me and told me that a plane hit the first tower and then another hit the second tower. Once I knew what was happening I started worrying about the people that died, and then the news really began to sink in. When I turned on the radio and they started talking about Muslims, I felt even worse.

Salima

I woke up on September 11, and turned on the television, to find the images of the twin towers on fire on every news channel. Then I saw the second plane go into the second tower. I was horrified. I sat, tears running down my face, praying for those who were losing their lives. I too watched television all day. I was actually in the midst of working on this project and writing this book. I called my professor and started to cry. I told her, I was scared for "my people." Muslims all around the world were going to be hurt by this. I felt so many things. Grieving for the loss of lives I had to witness, even if it was via television, and incredibly scared for the backlash to come. Violence and war were confronting me in ways they never had before, living in the sheltered reality of Canadian suburbia.

Major America television and radio networks complied with Bush Administration requests to edit or suppress statements opposing US military action.

Free speech TV internet posting
22nd Sept 2001

What were the immediate responses to September 11 in terms of who was involved? And what was your response? What rhetoric, language and concepts were used?

Amber

Osama bin Laden was named chief suspect pretty early on and I remember being surprised by that. If they knew so much about him and that he was such a threat, why didn't they stop him earlier?

It also became evident that this was a "crusade" of the West against the East. This was the language President Bush adopted (in addition to cowboy-on-the-hunt lingo). The concept was astonishingly and alarmingly simple, "You are either with us or you are against us." As if the world and struggles and wars really are black and white.

Farah

The immediate response was fear and hatred towards Islam, Muslim people and other minorities (for example, the Sikh man who was pulled off a bus). Bush's first speech was filled with anger and thoughts of revenge and hate. The captions on CNN were "America Strikes Back," trying to rile up not only the Americans, but other "freedom-loving people" to support Bush in the invasion of Afghanistan. After the first speech, I'm assuming his writers decided he should not be able to speak his mind any longer, because all of a sudden his words were very different. Now, Islam was not a violent religion, and the people in Afghanistan were not all terrorists. Now, everyone in the US should donate one dollar towards aid for the children in Afghanistan. We watched the world leaders unite (all of a sudden, Tony Blair was a very important figure, when two days earlier, not many people even knew his name) against this "war against democracy and all that is good."

Nazneen

"Terrorist Attack"-those were the words that we heard over and over again. These words were spread by the media and were accepted by everyone around me. Connections were being made not just with Osama Bin Laden, but also with Islam. For example, there was a

The Pentagon, reacting to reports of heavy civilian casualties in its bombing raids, spent millions of tax-payers dollars purchasing highly accurate satellite images of civilians in Afghanistan in order to prevent their release to the Western media.

Major networks released guidelines on reporting civilian casualties in Afghanistan ordering that reports of new civilian deaths must be balanced with reminders of the 9-11 attacks.

Free speech TV internet posting
22nd Sept 2001

The Merciful

news report that they found a car at the border in which, they said, there was a Qur'an. So now everything had Islam attached to it. Islamic terms, such as jihad and Qur'an were thrown around, so frequently that it made me sick to hear them.

Salima

The response of the US government was: "I think you hit me, and even if you didn't, you look like you would, so I am going to hit you back." The big bully found a smaller, defenceless enemy, and it was Afghanistan. The argument that they were going after the Taliban offered little consolation when blood was spilled all over Afghanistan. The whole point was to find Bin Laden and instead they found down-trodden people, clutching for existence, having already suffered hunger, displacement and injustice for over twenty years, who now became collateral damage. And let's not forget the oil the US can have access to if they "save" the Afghans.

Toronto Stats: Hate Crimes increased by 66 percent in Toronto, reported by Metro Toronto Police.

Hate crimes, racism and Islamophobia: The aftermath of September 11 for Muslims and other minoritized groups.

Farah

I wish I could say I was surprised, but I wasn't. If anything, as soon as I saw the buildings go down, I braced myself for the hate crimes that were about to come. I was angry when I heard of the Muslim woman who had her hijab torn off. I was even angrier when mosques were defaced and set on fire. These were the obvious symbols of Islam and, therefore, the targets. If I'm going to be completely honest, I think that if I was on the other side, if I was a non-Muslim, average middle-class person in Canada, I would have been furious towards Islam and Muslim people in general. If I was watching all the media coverage of Bush and his harsh words and seeing the despair of the fire workers and the family members of those working in the World Trade Center I would be angry too. If I had no idea what Islam was about and my only source of information was CNN, I too would blame a religion that I knew nothing about, except that it preaches violence.

Nazneen

I have seen so much hatred on the streets, hatred from those you are around every day.

Amber

Canadian Muslims have been experiencing violence. The events of September 11 have opened the doors of suspicion on Muslim Canadians. I wonder whose side you are on? Does that woman in hijab support Islamic fanaticism? Do the Muslims in your community endorse the actions of terrorists? Some residents in the small town north of Toronto where my parents live are asking these kinds of questions.

Salima

Hate crimes and discrimination against Muslims and Arabs or anyone perceived to be Muslim or associated with Islam increased after September 11. The Toronto police stated that hate crimes increased by 66% in Toronto. I heard of a young boy from western Ontario who was hung in a schoolyard by his former friends. Another boy was mocked and attacked by his young friends because his name is Osama. A woman wearing the hijab was yelled at in the subway. I heard about other women, wearing the hijab, for whom the bus drivers would not stop. Colleagues would look at Muslims with suspicion. People were denied jobs because of their names. I remember that for weeks after September 11 police cars would circle around or be in the parking lot of our jamat khana. What were they looking for? Were they there for "protection," and if so, whose protection exactly? There was racial profiling at airports, on the streets, changes to immigration policies to "protect" the country from "those" people. Let's not forget the fact that Sikhs were attacked because they wear turbans and Hindu temples were burned down. Anyone perceived to be Muslim (whatever that means) was a possible suspect.

The impact of all of this? Muslim women did not (and do not) leave their homes out of fear; children at school wanted (want) to change their names and deny their identities; Muslims felt (feel) that they had to carry the burden of others' wrongdoing; Muslims had no public or private safe spaces or places; they suffered depression, stress, shame,

In September, a few days before the attack on New York, the US energy information administration reported that Afghanistan's significance from an energy standpoint stems from its geographical position as a potential transit route for oil and natural gas exports from Central Asia to the Arabian Sea. This includes possible oil and natural gas export and pipelines through Afghanistan.

George Monibot. In the *Guardian*
October 22, 2001

alienation and disconnection from the country they call home; they felt a distrust of national institutions and their fellow citizens. Let's not water down the feelings and experiences of many Muslims by talking about the support and friendship that came out of this, as important as they were.

Why did it happen?

Amber

Wow, this is a loaded question. I have to say first that there is no justification for violence. Maybe in my cushy, protected life here in Canada I can say that, but I believe it. However, I think that when people are oppressed for a long time, eventually they will snap. Is this a case of you reap what you sow? Probably. It's been shown that Osama Bin Laden was a product of the US, that the US supplied weapons and training to the Mujahedeen to fight the Russians; so Osama and his like came with their own principles (however misguided) and bit the hand that fed them.

Farah

This happened for a number of reasons, I think. However, in my opinion, religious reasons are last on the list. I think that people are tired of the United States as the dictator of the world. It amazes me that while the US may be a democracy, it appears that the planet earth is a dictatorship, with Bush leading us all.

Salima

I think there are many angles from which we can examine this question. Some say that it was Osama Bin Laden (though we have little substantiated evidence that it was him) getting back at America for its presence in the Middle East, in particular its involvement with Israel and the persecution of Palestinians, its presence in Saudi Arabia and for causing the suffering of Iraqis. There are others who say that Osama Bin Laden has his own political interests and that this is one way of making his interests known. Some believe this is a symbolic fight against the spread of Western hegemony, and yet others say that people around the world have had enough of American dominance and involvement in the affairs of other countries and this was retaliation for more than the Middle East. One thing is for certain, if you oppress someone long enough, eventually he will either take his own life out of frustration or retaliate, and rightly so, for being so dehumanized and deprived of a dignified life.

There is no way to escape the fact that Muslims around the world have been dragged into this mess, that we have been further jarred into an awareness of violence, war and geopolitical issues.

Farah

Muslims need to unite. When the rest of the world is fighting us, why are we fighting each other? We are playing right into the US's plan to divide and conquer. It's really not that difficult. Today the US is friend to Pakistan, last week it was friend to Iran, the week before it was friend to Iraq. If all these countries became friends with one another, there would be no need for any US assistance. Shut off the oil. And then sit back and watch who the US attacks next. I don't think it will take long to see what their true motives are.

Amber

We nonviolent Muslims are silent when fanatics such as Bin Laden quote verses from the Qur'an that say "Slay [enemies] wherever you find them!" (4:89) We know very well that he is quoting selectively and has left out the directives to peace, which in almost every case, follow a passage regarding warfare: "Thus, if they let you be, and do not make war on you, and offer you peace, God does not allow you to harm them." (4:90) No matter how vehemently I say that Islam is not addicted to war, the truth is that it has been violently hijacked by violent fanatical practitioners.

Soon after September 11, I went to a mosque in Scarborough where the practitioners were also worried about fanaticism and the consequences of American retaliation for September 11. The imam began his sermon close to home, talking about community and telling the congregation that it needed to donate resources, money, clothing and blood - the Red Cross would set up a clinic at the mosque in three weeks. He spoke of the tragedy that was, as the terrorists claim, "done in the name of Islam," and how this was a clear contradiction of what Islam teaches. The imam spoke about the difficult effort that is required to put Allah's will into practice at every level of life -personal and social as well as political. As he began to speak of the joy of living in a multicultural country and of the challenge to work for peace, I was reminded of an extremely important and much-quoted tradition, which my father often mentions. Returning home from battle, Prophet Muhammad said to his companions: "We are returning from the lesser jihad to the greater jihad," that is, the far more important struggle to rid our hearts of evil.

Salima

Apathy is something that stands out for me. At times I can understand people not wanting to step out of their daily lives to speak out in society when things are so blatantly wrong, because they just want to survive or are afraid or are too busy. But no more, we can't afford to be apathetic, not physically, spiritually or psychologically.

The Bush Administration recently hired an ad executive to help "sell America" through a propaganda war in Afghanistan.

Free speech TV internet posting 22nd Sept 2001

I too remember going to jamat khana for guidance. What do I do? Can I help change this worsening situation for Muslims? I was a landfill of toxic and defeatist thoughts and emotions. Then I heard a speech from the Imam in which he spoke about the need for Muslims to speak without fear against hatred and ignorance about Islam and Muslims, to stand up and talk about the ethics of Islam and to challenge others to hear us. Without fear, he said, without fear, I thought. I felt rejuvenated.

I strongly feel that silence among Muslims needs to be broken, especially among progressive and forward-looking Muslims. Let's educate ourselves about world events, politics, human rights, economics, racism, development issues, and so on and be politically and socially conscious. We are so narrowly focused that we don't make broader links and in the process alienate ourselves and our causes. We need to think outside the boxes that we and society have created. Let's talk about and challenge the injustices in Muslim countries in the name of Islam and the injustices in Canada and the US in the name of democracy, self-preservation and national security.

Nazneen

Wherever I am I believe I am able to influence and challenge people's thinking. The places where I spend the most time, such as my home and at work, are where I feel I can make the most difference, by staying strong and speaking out against injustice in every moment of my existence, small or big. In my company alone, I have been able to make changes by speaking out against unfair treatment or narrow mindedness. This is a daily struggle that we can be engaged in without taking too much time out from our daily lives.

Larger context of violence and state-sponsored terrorism.

Amber

September 11 is a part of the more global and historical trend of terrorism that has been sponsored by a certain global superpower. I'm sure they do it deliberately to keep oil-rich states weak and unstable. Think about it, the superpower leaps into the country with troops to run out the evil dictator every few years, hence giving the appearance of "saving" the people. Then they continue to operate military bases in the oil-rich states and keep their fist in the pie and keep prospering from the black gold. At the same time, you have to wonder, why are they backing "fundamentalist militia" in a neighbouring state who might go AWOL on them in a couple of years? Is this foreign policy? Or a self-fulfilling prophecy?

Salima

How can we not see this in the context of a global history of violence perpetrated by the US? I was reading, *Why Do People Hate America?* by Ziauddin Sardar and Merryl Wynn Davies, and in it they describe a century of American intervention inflicting violence and repression, from atrocities in the US against the Native peoples, to East Asia, Eastern Europe, Latin America, and West Asia. How can we not consider September 11 within this history? We are talking about untold numbers of deaths and suffering caused by American policy, and actions. On September 11, 3,000-5,000 people died. How many people have died at the hands of the US in the last 114 years? The blood can't ever be washed away.

The Merciful

Responding to the war in Iraq.

It is disheartening that violence is still used to gain peace. What a contradiction! Billions of taxpayer dollars are spent on the military machine--this does not give the impression that we are working towards peace at all. In fact, we are living on the offensive and defensive. Who is the enemy we must protect ourselves from? Who is it that needs to be protected? Who gets to decide who does the protecting? Big questions, which at the moment are posed in such a way that the answer seems simple. The Protector: the United States. The Enemy: anyone who poses a threat to their power and expansion. Noam Chomsky has outlined the essence of the National Strategy Report of the United States, reiterating this very point, "that the US will rule the world by force, which is the dimension-the only dimension-in which it is supreme. Furthermore, it will do so for the indefinite future, because if any potential challenge arises to US domination, the US will destroy it before it becomes a challenge." Given the fact that there is no opposing world power at present, the domination and superiority of the United States may be contested, but for the most part will not be stopped.

This brings us to the current status of Iraq. We have just lived through the attack on Iraq by the US. The reasoning for the war began with what was deemed as Iraq's refusal to get rid of their weapons of mass destruction (which have yet to be found). This impetus transformed into new rhetoric about liberating Iraq from the tyranny of Saddam. Let's also state that Saddam is no peace-loving hero. He has done his share of damage to people's lives. The incredible plight of the Shias and Kurds cannot be forgotten. However, it seems unlikely that the US would focus their efforts on Iraq for the sheer liberation of humanity. If that were the case, then why not focus on their own home-grown problems of poverty and violence? Why spend billions of dollars to save "other" people?

The answer lies in what the gains are for the US, in attacking Iraq. The Middle East is a region that poses a threat to US economic expansionism. It is important to destabilize any regimes that pose a threat to America's control of oil. Iraq, one of the weakest Arab states, was an easy target, a good sell to show the world that the US is now entering a new phase of American internationalism. The economic and ideological gains are huge. Responsiblity for the reconstruction of Iraq has been given to American companies. Media outlets were set up before the war, but since then it is no surprise that American media conglomerates will have dominion. So the liberation of Iraq has a particular look and feel, one that was predetermined. It is the transformation of Iraqis into consumers of American ideals, way of life, and perception of the world. The transformation of the Middle East is well on its way.

In the midst of all this, frustration grows on the part of Iraqis, because on the one hand Saddam is gone, but on the other hand the country is now in the possession of the US. An outside source that knows little about the culture, the people, and the history of that region will "assist" in setting up a government that nicely supports the "allies." This volcano of frustration also lies among other Arabs and Muslims, who feel they have little recourse to stop what seems like a bowling ball slowly toppling one pin at a time. Who is next? Iran? Syria? Perhaps this is not a religious fight, but it is "Islamic Extremism" that the US is fighting after all.

Muslims can't help but feel that this is an attack on Islam and Muslims. Will the reconstruction of Iraq involve religious leaders and considerations of religious importance? For the majority Muslim populations, the complete uprooting of religion will stir up bitter feelings and will only encourage those who may want to enforce oppressive Islamic interpretations and practices. And for those Muslims not living in the Middle East, who oppose American occupation and American expansion, the inability to influence US decision-making is also frustrating.

It is a grim time. What is needed is to find spaces where dissent can trickle down and bring changes. The responsibility lies not only on the subversive, but also with those who straddle the middle way, those who are a part of mainstream institutions and decision-making. Iraq should not be repeated. That possibility should be enough for us to be asking what we need to do differently to bring about a different future.

Death Toll Estimates in Iraq as of 23 April.
Iraqi civilians-1,252 killed; 5,103 injured (Iraqi estimate); 1,878-2,325 killed
(The Iraq Body Count Organization estimate)
From the *Guardian Limited* on-line

Significant dates concerning Iraq.

16 July 1979
Saddam Hussein becomes president of Iraq, after engineering the resignation of President Hasan al-Bakr.

22 September 1980
Border dispute between Iran and Iraq escalates into full-scale war.

6 August 1990
UN imposes economic sanctions on Iraq.

16 January 1991
Gulf War starts. US-led coalition begins air strikes against Iraq.

6 April 1991
Iraq accepts UN resolution requiring it to end production of weapons of mass destruction and to allow monitoring by the UN special commission inspection team (UNSCOM).

27 June 1993
US conducts air strikes against Iraqi intelligence service, in retaliation for assassination plot against former president George Bush.

14 April 1995
"Oil-for-food" programme begins, allowing Iraq to export oil to buy food and medicine.

July 1995
Iraq threatens to withdraw cooperation with inspectors unless some sanctions and oil embargo are lifted by 31 August.

21 June 1997
UN demands Iraq allow inspection teams access to disputed sites.

23 February 1998
Iraq promises UN Secretary-General Kofi Annan unrestricted access for UN inspectors.

16 December 1998
UN inspection team is withdrawn, after concluding that Iraq is not cooperating fully.

16–19 December 1998
Operation "Desert Fox" begins: four days of US-British air strikes against Iraqi weapons programmes.

15 February 2001
US and Britain bomb Iraq's air defence network.

30 January 2002
In the first State of the Union address after the September 11 attacks on America, US president George Bush says Iraq is part of an "axis of evil."

1 August 2002
Iraq invites UN chief weapons inspector to Baghdad.

12 September 2002
President Bush addresses UN to present the case for war against Iraq

16 September 2002
Iraq accepts "unconditional" return of UN inspectors.

16 October 2002
Iraq renews offer to UN weapons inspectors, after "referendum" gives Saddam Hussein another seven-year term as president with 100% of the vote.

8 November 2002
UN security council votes unanimously to back a US-British resolution requiring Iraq to reinstate weapons inspectors after a four year absence.

13 November 2002
President Saddam sends a letter to the UN Secretary-General Annan, accepting the UN resolution.

18 November 2002
United Nations weapons inspectors arrive in Baghdad to re-launch the search for weapons of mass destruction.

2 December 2002
The British government publishes a dossier documenting human rights abuses in Iraq. It is attacked by Amnesty International for being "opportunistic and selective." Critics say it uses longstanding human rights abuses to achieve current military goals, and ignores US and UK support for Saddam at the time of some of the worst atrocities.

17 December 2002
Colin Powell, the US Secretary of State, hints that the White House will reject the Iraqi weapons declaration, saying there were problems with the 12 000-page document.

19 December 2002
The United States accuses Baghdad of being in "material breach" of the UN resolution after the UN's chief weapons inspector, Hans Blix, says the Iraqi arms declaration contains little new information about its weapons of mass destruction capability.

30 December 2002

It emerges that the Reagan administration and its special Middle East envoy, Donald Rumsfeld, did little to stop Iraq developing weapons of mass destruction in the 1980s, even though they knew Saddam Hussein was using chemical weapons "almost daily" against Iran.

31 December 2002

A UN inspection team member in Iraq admits to finding "zilch" evidence of weapons of mass destruction and says that the teams have been provided with little guidance from western intelligence agencies.

9 January 2003

Hans Blix says UN weapons inspectors have not found any "smoking guns" in their search for weapons of mass destruction in Iraq, but acknowledges that Iraq's 12 000 page weapons declaration was incomplete.

13 January 2003

In his monthly televised briefing, Tony Blair says that weapons of mass destruction will reach terrorists and that Britain could act against Iraq with the US without a second UN resolution.

19 January 2003

The US offers President Saddam immunity from prosecution if his departure from Baghdad would avert war.

6 February 2003

Around 100 aircraft and 7 000 RAF personnel are to be deployed in the build up for a possible war against Iraq, the defence secretary, Geoff Hoon, announces.

9 February 2003

The US reacts furiously to a Franco-German peace initiative to triple the number of arms inspectors in Iraq and back them up with surveillance flights. The Bush administration sees it as a thinly-disguised attempt to derail the US timetable for war.

15 February 2003

Anti-war protesters take to the streets of London and cities around the world. Around one million people march through the British capital to hear speakers, including Jesse Jackson, address the crowds in Hyde Park, in what is the UK's biggest-ever protest. More than 50 000 gather in Glasgow.

24 February 2003
Russia, France and Germany put forward a counter-proposal to America and Britain's draft resolution: a step-by-step programme for Iraqi disarmament. The Turkish cabinet strikes a deal with America to allow US troops to be deployed there in exchange for a billion-dollar aid package, but it still has to be passed by the Turkish parliament. Meanwhile, the first consignment of NATO equipment to defend Turkey from an attack by Iraq in the event of war arrives.

28 February 2003
Hans Blix's interim report to the UN is published, giving a mixed assessment of Iraqi cooperation with weapons inspectors, but hailing Saddam Hussein's commitment to comply with tomorrow's UN deadline for the destruction of Iraq's illegal Samoud 2 missiles.

2 March 2003
It emerges that Britain and the US have been increasing their air strikes on Iraq in recent days, in an apparent bid to "soften up" the country's defences ahead of a war.

6 March 2003
In a nationwide television address, the US President Bush indicates that war is very close.

11 March 2003
The US defence secretary, Donald Rumsfeld, causes a political storm after suggesting America could attack President Saddam alone. Blair later stresses Britain will fight alongside the US in any attack.

17 March 2003
With China, France and Russia opposed to an attack, the US and UK abandon hope of gaining security council support for a second resolution authorising war on Iraq. They withdraw the resolution, blaming the French veto threat.

20 March 2003
War begins.

18 April 2003
Tens of thousands of Iraqis demonstrate against the US occupation of Iraq in central Baghdad.

Timeline extracted from *The Guardian Unlimited*. For complete timeline please refer to following site:
http://www.guardian.co.uk/Iraq/page/0,12438,793802,00.html

There are so many people that have died from atrocities and war worldwide. Here are some numbers. These numbers may not reflect total numbers in each country.

Iraq: According to the 21 March 1998 *Times Union* (Albany), the UN Food and Agriculture Organization estimated that 1,000,000 Iraqis, incl. 560,000 children, died as a result of malnutrition and disease caused by the international embargo imposed following the invasion of Kuwait.

Bosnia: (*NY Times Magazine*, 23 April 1995): 25,000 to 60,000

Somalia: 50,000 killed in fighting and 300,000 dead of starvation (in 23 months following Jan. 1991)

Nicaragua: (1972-91) 50,000 (Chomsky 1987) Contra Rebellion (1981-90): 30,000 (*Washington Post*, 6 Feb. 1990)

Afghanistan: 20 May 2002 [London] *Guardian*: Max. war-related avoidable deaths: 49,600

Chechnya, 1994-99 Both Wars: 11 Nov. 2002 *Time*: 38,000 combatants + 200,000 civilians

Tajikstan, Civil War (1992-96) *War Annual* 8 (1997): 40,000

Kashmir & Jammu, Civil War (1989 et seq.) *Times of India*, (6 January 2001) Total since 1990: 26,421

Peru, 1980-99 *SIPRI* 1988: 28,000 (1981-96)

Sri Lanka (1977-) *Ploughshares* 2000: 60-100,000

Rwanda (1994-5, primarily Tutsi killed by Hutu) Victoria Brittain, *Death of Dignity* (1998): 850,000

Iran-Iraq War (1980-88) *Timeframe*: 1,200,000 (900,000 Iranians and 300,000 Iraqis)

Information from: **http://users.erols.com/mwhite28/warstat2.htm**

We are the spirits of the great women before us

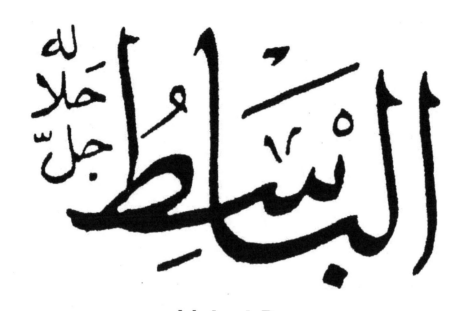

Majlis al-Bâsit

The Expander

Allah doth wish to make clear to you and to show you the ordinances of those before you; and (He doth wish to) turn to you (In Mercy). And Allah is All-knowing, All-wise.

(4.26)

Cultural work, storytelling and connecting through projects such as these offer ways for us, as marginalized groups, to be heard and to reclaim our power to tell our life histories. Our children and our communities desperately need to hear these stories and to find role models who can articulate the issues they face and offer hope for the future. As Muslims, people of colour and women, we are always searching for visible women of colour we can learn from. Female role models and stories told by women are rare. We did not want this book to tell only the stories of the women in the project. We wanted to take it a step further, like a tree with many branches that expand and are connected to other branches. We want to share our role models with you, those Muslim women from whom we have learned, and who have inspired us. These stories and this knowledge can then connect the women in our group to the women in their lives, and then to you and the women in your lives. We hope these women can bring gifts into your life, as they have into ours.

Nazneen and her khala (aunt) Saeeda Choudhury

I would like to introduce you to my aunt, Saeeda Choudhury. She is one of the women I know who practises her religion and challenges it, too. I admire her humility, her respect for other religions, and her ability to stand up for justice. I have learned a lot from her. She says," God says you don't need anyone to find me." And she finds him every day.

Saeeda Choudhury

I was brought up in a Sunni Muslim family with Islamic rules such as regular prayer, reading of the Qur'an, and fasting during the month of Ramadan. One good thing was that our home was mostly open minded, without the influence of mullahs (religious leaders). Due to unfortunate family circumstances, I started to depend totally on God, and prayer became my means of peace. So many things I learned about Islam felt contradictory. From the age of sixteen my young brain searched for logic. When I asked questions about Islam, the answers from people were always frightening and difficult to understand.

One day I questioned my dad. His answers were simple and straightforward: "Remember God, be thankful and do right things." He was a great man, down-to-earth and, in many ways, he was a role model for me. After that, I never listened to anyone. I did whatever made sense to me. At twenty-two, I got married to a very special, wonderful man. But our life together began with problems, sharing two different cultures and personalities. In spite of this, we are glad to have been together for over forty years. As for sects, from my heart, I do not believe in them. If someone asks which sect I belong to, my answer is none. I am a Muslim, that's all. We all believe in one God and should respect one another. Everyone has to answer for his or her own deeds. If someone wants to correct you, they should first correct themselves. People could live together in peace if they followed this principle.

Our media represents the Muslim woman as oppressed, backward, forced to wear head scarves, not allowed to do what other women do, and so on. Some of these images are true to an extent. In the name of establishing Islamic societies, men have often targeted women. These men seem to believe God gave them the right to control women, to help women go to heaven. Some say that wives, sisters and daughters should sit at home, covered from head to foot, and stop all entertainment because it is haram (sin). Women living with men of Tabligh (preachers) often suffer the most.

On the other hand, many Muslim women are strong, educated, supporting families and working shoulder to shoulder with men, and they freely choose to cover themselves. Women have become national leaders in strict Muslim countries, such as Pakistan and Bangladesh. These are positive images of Muslim women that the media should consider.

I feel pain and sorrow for the women who are controlled by fanatics in the name of religion. This is happening in places like Afghanistan and Iran. These extremists give a bad name to Islam, practising the opposite of its teachings. The Muslim community can be greatly helped by education and following the paths of Muslim scholars such as Rifat Hassan and Asma Jehangir who fight for the rights of Muslim women all over the world. These scholars help women to stand up for themselves and teach men the right path.

Islam affected my life profoundly. I am very proud to be a Muslim. It was Islam, my complete surrender to God Almighty, which made me strong, confident, patient. The purpose of my life is to care, share, and help. I try to remember my faults and to correct myself.

This teaches me to be aware of God and seek knowledge, no matter who or where it comes from. I love the company of wise, intelligent, open-minded people. All of this is a blessing of my religion. If we all think in such a way, with care and positive attitudes for other human beings despite sect or religion, Inshallah, we can make a strong community and help each other in our daily lives. We can all bring change to our social lives.

Amber and her mother Qaisra Nasrulla
The strongest woman I know is my mother, Qaisra Nasrulla, at whose feet heaven resides. Why? Her faith is unflappable: she believes in Islam. She has a commitment to the community in which she lives, finding time to volunteer dozens of hours at a local cancer hospital. She is the bedrock of our family. She supports us intellectually, emotionally and religiously, and unconditionally offers her guidance.

In the stream of words with my Ummi (mum) (Qaisra):
"Guidance doesn't end when you reach adulthood, it continues until the parent dies." Ouch! I don't like her to say that.

Qaisra Nasralla

Amber: Are there things about Islam that make you tense?

Qaisra: I wouldn't call it tension. It's more that sometimes it felt hard to guide your children, when you were being bombarded with thousands of images from outside. You've had certain experiences that you would not have had were you growing up in an Islamic country. There's the loss of language to contend with. You can read Arabic but you can't understand it word for word.

Amber: How do you think Islam will fare here?

Qaisra: I hate to say it but I think that it is doomed in Western society unless we Muslims band together under the banner of Islam, until we stop arguing among ourselves. We are the weakest link. (Laughter). Seriously, we need to defend Muslim nations intellectually rather than with force. We are intelligent and we are strong, but we need a strategy and then as a people we can overcome anything.

Amber: It sounds a bit dire. How do you stay positive?

Qaisra: Prayer. I talk to God and know that one day he will listen. I live in hope. But you're asking me all these questions and you should know that from day to day I don't think of these things, I just go on with my life. I don't see that I'm a better person than people here just because I'm Muslim. It's about how we behave towards others.

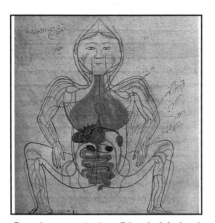

Circulation of the Blood Medical
Manuscript 1SC

Topkapi Palace Museum

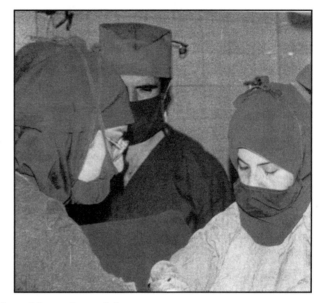

Zaynab and her role models

I do not find myself inspired by any one particular Muslimah. In my ongoing process of growth, I am more inspired by Muslimahs from different sects, ages, backgrounds, professions whom I meet face-to-face, on the internet and through books. I am inspired by women who demonstrate my ideals. I am inspired by women who set their standards within Islam and its meaning. I become inspired by different web sites put together by Muslimahs for Muslimahs. There they share questions and concerns as well as lessons and stories, they are women who stay home, women who work, women who wear or don't wear the hijab. Each encounter is unique and I take from it a piece that is unique, as no two women are alike.

Farah and her sister Tasleem.
I'd like to introduce you to one of the strongest women I know, my sister and half my soul, Tasleem Murji. I chose to interview Tasleem because she is motivated, compassionate, ambitious, focused, independent, altruistic and intelligent. She really lives her life as though she's an ambassador of Allah, and I admire and learn from that.

Tasleem Murji

Perhaps the ideal answer for every Muslim to the question, "What role does Islam play in your life?" should be, "Islam is my life." I'm not sure that I would say this. I would say that Islam shapes my life. It does this by defining my major pursuit in this world. Thus, Islam influences the choices that I make, since they serve as stepping stones to that final destination I long to reach.

It is important to express why I embrace Islam. It is my love for God and the belief that every living entity is a creation and a part (perhaps even an extension) of God. I feel the ethics of Islam allow me to love God and God's creation. So when I have to decide whether or not it is okay to lie to someone, or whether or not I should help a stranger, or whether or not I should wake up for class in the morning, I think of Allah. I employ the ethics of Islam to help me make my decisions. I practise the rituals of Islam to teach myself the discipline it takes to be committed to something. What makes me most excited about Islam is that I am allowed to think, in fact I am encouraged to think. Whether I am studying world history, or Einstein's Theory of Relativity, I am asking questions, and I am learning about Allah.

Salima and her Grandmother ~ Rupa Mandhan.

I thought long and hard about the women I consider to be my role models and I am proud to say that there are many. But when I ponder the women closest to me, I realize that I come from a long line of strong, incredible women. So, I want to share with you a line of women in my family, who have inspired me, given me hope and have always been a motivation for the work I have done and will continue to do. I tell you the story of my grandmother, who is our guiding light and an example of an extraodinary Muslim woman.

Rupa Bai Mandhan

My nani (my mother's mother), Rupa Mandhan, set the tone for the women who were to come in her family. In June 1994 my grandmother was dying. We had been informed by the doctors that she had cancer and did not have much time to live. As she lay in her hospital bed, eased by the nearness of death, she smiled and did not speak of her physical pain.

I was sitting at her beside during those last days of her life and she shared with me something I will never forget. She looked at me with her kind, deep eyes, took my hand and said, "Salima, don't be sad. I am leaving this world to enter the home I was separated from. This is a time for celebration, not for sorrow."

I heard these words and gasped for breath, as though hit by something magical.

My nani always had faith in a greater reality, in her boundless love for Allah. And yet again she had reminded me of our eternal nature.

My grandmother grew up in the early 1900s in Ahmadabad, Gujarat, in India. She had many siblings and came from a rural background. She had very little education but in her later life, after moving to UK, she learned English. She worked very hard to help her family. Her husband passed away and left her to take care of her seven children.

She was known to stand up for the rights of her daughters and other women, and spoke out against their mistreatment. Once, she heard that a man was abusing his wife and had threatened to kill her. My grandmother promptly hopped on a truck and travelled overnight to reach the woman's home. She pounded on the door and told the woman's husband that if anything happened to his wife he would have her to deal with. At that time this was extraordinary.

Her philanthropic work was devoted to women and women's issues. My nani moved to East Africa after marriage, but kept close ties with her homeland, most of which involved philanthropic work for girl children in Bombay.

My family left Uganda in 1972 when the dictator Idi Amin expelled South Asians from the country, giving them ninety days to leave. My family fled to UK, leaving behind all their belongings and their home. They ended up as refugees, with nothing but the clothes on their backs. Over time Nani and some other family members settled in UK, while others moved to Canada.

Being further away from her origins did not prevent her from committing her life to the disenfranchised in India. She helped orphan girls in India by visiting every year and saving a portion of her money to help sustain their orphanage. She was not a wealthy woman by any means and lived with the bare minimum necessities. She spent time with the girls and got to know many of them closely. She did this work for years, until she could no longer travel.

When I was in India in 1999, I went to visit this orphanage with my mother. Before I got there, I had no idea the degree to which my grandmother had dedicated her life to the girls. A swarm of girls came rushing to the gate as we walked in. They looked up at us, giggling shyly, hiding faces behind their hands. They told me about "Rupa Ma" and how much they enjoyed her visits. They talked about her unconditional love and generosity and how much they missed her. They said she always left a sense of hope behind when she left.

My grandmother stood for two things that were intimately connected: her faith in the Ultimate and her commitment to helping others. She lived selflessly, each moment inspired by the truth of her purpose, which was to be involved in peoples' struggles and to give of herself in whatever way she could.

I see my nani's light in my mother, in my sisters, in my nieces and in me. She is now gone to her home and I pray that she is happy there.

Munira and Fatima Takache

Fatima Takache is a Muslim woman, wife, mother, educator and community activist. She is the founder of an Islamic pre-school in Canada. Her students have excelled at an incredible rate in all areas: language (Arabic and English), art, expression, physical and social development. Every member of her family is an example of a good Muslim. She is my role model because she is the core of the family, providing them with a strong foundation.

Fatima Takache

Munira: What role does Islam play in your life?

Fatima: Actually, everything I do involves Islam. If I really think about it, I breathe Islam. I consider every movement, thought and action according to Islam. How I treat people, my behaviour, my thoughts, are all in accord with Islam. Here are a few examples. When I am shopping, I observe my behaviour so that I am polite and courteous to the people I meet, and my actions represent how observing Muslims should act, such as not drawing too much attention to myself in my dress, my attitude, and so on. The meat I buy must be halal, the cost must not be over my budget or put me or my family in great debt, what I buy must not be a waste but be something that I need or will use. You see, it is all related to Islam.

Munira: What are the tensions that exist in a Muslim, particularly a woman in Islam?

Fatima: I believe this is personal in most circumstances. I am a Muslim woman who observes modest dress and wears a scarf. My experience has been very good and I have not faced any discrimination or bad encounters with people. I have studied in college and university in Canada, I have experienced the work environment, and I have not faced anything negative. I believe negative experiences can happen wherever you live, whether in a country where no one looks like you or one in which there are many people just like you.

Munira: What are your visions for Muslim women and the community at large?
Fatima: It might seem unrealistic because of the present state of our communities, most of them are new and there is much to overcome, but I believe that with the help of God we will get to a point where all Muslims will create communities that are peaceful, that are righteous members of the bigger Canadian community and that will hold true Islamic values.

My vision comes from knowing that there are many educated Muslim women and many more to come who will marry, and raise children who hold these values and live by them. Being a good practising Muslim in the West is a choice. In so-called Muslim countries, there are people who practise because they have to, because there is stigma if they are not like the others. But here in Canada, those pressures do not exist, at least not to the same degree. As the Muslims in Canada increase their level of commitment to Islam, we will be able to achieve the vision I predict.

Salwa and Helweh Juma

When asked to choose someone whom I consider to be my role model, I immediately thought of Sister Helweh Juma. She is an outstanding Muslim woman who inspires and enriches me in my spiritual pursuits. Since the time I was a child in her class, she has taught me much about our deen and about our duties in life as Muslims. She has been a source of guidance in my community and has served my generation intellectually, emotionally and, above all, spiritually.

Helweh Juma

I was born in a small village in Lebanon. I grew up on a farm, the eldest child in a family of eleven children, and was educated in Arabic and in English in my home village. I came to Canada in 1967, got married and had four children: three boys and one girl. I was a stay-at-home mom. But during that period and to this day, I was involved in the education system as an International Language teacher. That position started me off as a volunteer in the community in 1976. It was also the first Arabic and Islamic school for children. From 1978 I have been part of the International Language program with the North York Board of Education and the Toronto Board of Education. I wore my hijab until the age of fifteen in my village in Lebanon but then removed it due to social pressures within my own village, even though I was raised in a religious home. I subsequently came to Canada without the hijab, but then I started wearing it again in 1975. I adopted complete Muslim dress in 1980.

Now-when I look at myself-I am first a human being, then a woman, a daughter, a wife, a mother, and a grandmother and also a teacher, a court interpreter, a community outreach person and a friend. As you can see I wear different hats at different times and I am very comfortable with any role I need to be in at any time.

The Expander

My whole life is Islam-I eat, breathe, sleep, speak and work Islam. Anything I do is according to Islamic teaching, the Qur'an and the tradition of the Prophet (sallallaahu alayhe wasallam). I cannot imagine myself not living according to Islam. It is a very comfortable life for me. I am very grateful for the blessing of being born a Muslim and raised a Muslim and being able to live today as a Muslim.

As for existing tensions, particularly as a woman in Islam, I can't deny that fact. When I meet people for the first time, usually the first impression I get is that they are uncomfortable with the way I look. But as people get to know me and see what's inside, the tension seems to ease away. They become understanding and appreciative and some of them are surprised that someone who looks Muslim can be intelligent, interesting, knowledgeable and friendly, in other words, a living, breathing human being.

I have a lot of hopes and much anticipation for the new generation of Muslim women. Perhaps it's because I have been involved in their upbringing for the past thirty-five years or so through education and community outreach. However, I think that their task will be different than my generation's; they will be university-educated professionals and social activists. Some may enter the political arena. They will bring into the picture, I would hope, the best of both worlds. They will be able to bridge the gap that maybe our generation did not have the knowledge or ability to bridge. I hope and pray that our children don't have the baggage that my older generation brought with them from their cultures and backgrounds, so that they can feel like one ummah. They mustn't say, "I am Arab Canadian" or "I am Pakistani Canadian" but that they are Canadian Muslims, believing men and women. This hopefully will strengthen their bond as the new generation here. We should also encourage the young people to marry within Islam and build the new family that hopefully will be more successful in its endeavour to help build a better and safer world for us all.

I think the issues of leadership, identity, unity and even reaching out to the universe at large are indeed the challenges at this point in our history. Islam is a religion for all. We should always remember what Allah (swt) said about Prophet Muhammad, (saw): "You have been sent as mercy to all humankind." So Muhammad and his message and the Qur'an are not just for Muslims, Arabs or Pakistanis, but for the whole human race. We are supposed to follow in the footsteps of the Prophet (sallallaahu alayhe wa sallam) and bring this mercy to the universe, to everyone. We have the opportunity here to live among the people of the book-those who can understand where we are coming from and those with whom we have a lot of things we can agree upon. We Muslims, Christians and Jews have that base for interaction, for a relationship, for mutual respect and understanding. Islam is defined, here and abroad, as an act of worship, a ritual, a tradition. But Islam is much more than that-it is a way of life. Islam is active, not passive. To be a Muslim is to be productive, not just within your family and your home, but also within your neighbourhood and your community at large. When I say community at large, I am not talking about the Arab community, the Pakistani community or the Muslim community. I am talking about the human community, the human race. There is the element of worship in Islam, which is the relationship between the servant and Allah. But there is also the relationship between human and human, which is encouraged in Islam. When we look at the Rasul (saw), his wife, his companions, his family and followers, how were they instrumental in the spreading of Islam east and west? Not just by acts of worship but also because they were rulers, professionals, warriors, and social activists. Therefore we need to look at this very deeply, and take that part of the religion and practise it here where we are all living. We should take the opportunity to interact with others and show them the true spirit of Islam. Otherwise our duty in this world has not been fulfilled.

I thank Allah, (swt), for the opportunity to be part of this project. I admire Sister Salima for doing this book and I hope she continues to have success. We need more projects like this one. May Allah bless all the women who have participated in this project.

The Expander

Mezghan and her mother

My role model is my mother. I admire her courage in facing all the difficulties of her life. Through her actions she became a role model for her children.

Mrs. Hakimy

When I was very small my father, who was away at work, was called to go to war. He was not even allowed to come home to see his family first. We were all in a state of shock, because anything could happen in war. My mother not only had to support our family financially now but also had to fulfill the responsibilities of both parents. She had to take care of us, emotionally support us and give us courage to deal with our father's absence. She smiled even when she was sad, so we would not know her pain and problems. She fed us first, even giving us her portion of food. She worked outside and inside the home and sent us to school. In spite of her many responsibilities, she managed to take time to teach us how to live in the light of our faith.

She has provided an example of courage and wisdom for me to follow. Throughout her many challenging and difficult times she never gave up hope. She raised her children, giving them love, care, and support. She gave them the confidence to believe in themselves, to stand on their own and fight for themselves. She had a firm belief in herself and her faith and she taught her children how to cope with difficulties through her examples. She has always been a great supporter of me. Whatever I have achieved and will achieve is because of my mother.

Muslim women and role models.

Fatima al Zahra (a s): The daughter of Prophet Muhammad (pbuh) and Khadija (a s).

She was given the title "Leader of the ladies of the worlds" by her father. She was an inspiring woman because she was the spiritual mother of the faithful ones. She had a lot of her father's traits, including nobility and kindness. She married Imam Ali (a s). Her life was very short: she died at eighteen. Her husband prepared her body for burial and fulfilled her last wish of not letting anyone know where she was laid to rest. Fatima al Zahra (a s) was loved greatly by her father. She and Imam Ali (a s) had two sons, Imam Hassan and Imam Hussain, in addition to Muhsin who was premature and did not survive. They had two daughters, Zainab and Umm Kulthum, peace and blessings be upon them all.

Rabi'a Al-Adawiyya

Rabi'a is considered to be the greatest of the mystic saints in Islam. She lived in the early days of Islam, having been born in Basra, in 717. Praised by her predecessors and those saints who lived in her time, Rabi'a reached a level of devotion to God that was unparalleled and that many longed to reach. She was able to inspire great mystics such as Farid-u-din Attar, who wrote extensively about Rabi'a. She committed her life and love to God. She taught both men and women about the ways of love and God and inspired them with her commitment and piety. Here is a prayer she used to say, which reflects her life and vision.

Oh my God, my concern and my desire in this world is that I should remember Thee above all the things of this world, and in the next, that out of all who are in that world, I should meet with Thee alone. This is what I would say, "Thy will be done."

Bibi Zaynab (a s)

The Holy Prophet's daughter Hadrat Fatima (a s) and Imam Ali (a s), cousin of the Prophet gave birth to a little girl. Of her physical appearance little is known. Some people remarked that she appeared as a "shining sun" and a "piece of the moon." In Medina it was Zaynab's practice to hold regular meetings for women in which she shared her knowledge and taught them the precepts of the deen of Islam as laid out in the Holy Qur'an. Her gatherings were well and regularly attended. She had the reputation as an inspiring teacher among the women. Zaynab (a.s.) was also nicknamed Zahidah (abstemious) and Abidah (devoted). After the killing of Imam Hussain (a s), Bibi Zaynab and the other women were taken prisoner and brought to the palace court of Yazid. It was here where she provoked emotion with her sermon and condemnation of what had happened. Had it not been for Zaynab (a.s), we would not have known the objectives of the qiyam of Hussain.

Bibi Zaynab Masjid (mosque) containing her shrine Damascus, Syria

Through hope we gift the world with vision.

Majlis al-Hâdi
The Guide

One Day every soul will come up struggling for itself, and every soul will be recompensed (fully) for all its actions, and none will be unjustly dealt with.

(16:111)

Voicing our visions and hopes for our future is a fundamental step in shaping our lives and communities. Unfortunately, as women living in societies dominated by patriarchy our visions and hopes are often relegated to the periphery of the dominant culture's concerns. In fact, our contributions to our communities and society are often marginalized and unheard. Women's central role in their communities' development is paramount for healthier, just and equitable societies. Their visions and desires for themselves, their communities and the world at large must be heard. They must be taken seriously. The women in this group describe what they desire for themselves and for their communities and societies. In this way they claim their place and right in this world.

The Guide

Visions and hopes.

Farah

For myself. I want to leave this world knowing that I did all that I could do. I think that's going to be in the area of gender, because that is where my passion is.

For my community. I pray that the social programs we have in place continue and we get ourselves out there and continue to make attempts to connect with the rest of the Muslim ummah.

Nazneen

For myself. I want to know more, I still have a lot to learn. There are many things I am unsure about. I crave knowledge. I would like to see myself more involved with communities. I think they need a little shake somehow.

For my community. I don't see much hope for my community. I pray that the new generations realize the problems. The youth are ashamed of their identity; they live in a world of illusion and it may be too late for them. They need role models.

Munira

For myself. I want to acquire enough knowledge about religion and Islam specifically and someday get my PhD. That is a long process, it may not happen for another seven to ten years. Sometimes I wonder about the way I dress; there is no misinterpretation as I am completely covered. I picture myself at the University of Toronto in complete black abaya (full black veil, leaving only the eyes to be seen) speaking to a group of students and them thinking this is nothing like what I thought you would be, dressed the way you are. So maybe it's a shock factor, but I do feel a certain serenity being dressed like that.

For my community. A lot more has to be done in terms of community activism. How can we use Islam when we are doing environmental activism and social activism? We need to make sure that we don't put Islam on the back burner and that we talk about Islam. At the moment we are afraid to bring it up because we want to normalize ourselves, to make people think we are just like them. We have to stop doing that, because Islam is rich with many lessons. I would like to see more community activism. It will be essential for us to come together, put aside some of our differences, and show that we are united.

Zaynab

For myself. I want to educate myself more and seek more Islamic knowledge and be able to apply it. I have a lot of inner tension and anger I have to deal with, particularly with regards to men. I would like to wear the hijab, because that will mean that I don't care what people think I look like. My glasses, my bun and my long skirts have been my hijab and I see that people see me differently and approach me with a little more respect. In terms of my future and my kids I hope to pass Islam on to them and to be more open minded.

For the community. I think everything starts at home. As a community, we need to be more aware of this and take more responsibility for our children. Inshallah, let's bring up children who can be good.

Maha

For myself. My hope for myself as a Muslim woman is to be true to the understanding of Islam that I have achieved. My fear is that I am going to be so frustrated with the communities, so disillusioned by the garbage, that I may turn my back on my faith. Inshallah I won't, but it's a fear that I have. My faith is so important to me that I don't think I could ever do that. I don't think I could ever cut myself off from the divine. It's too crucial an aspect of who I am.

For my community. My hope for my community is that people of my own age become aware of history and have access to knowledge that we don't have access to. I am talking about the widespread knowledge that could change everything-the way we view each other, ourselves, our faith, the way we practise. There shouldn't be impediments placed in their way. I hope that this knowledge is disseminated on a wide scale.

Salima

For myself. I pray that I can live, act and be in God. I pray that all the work that I do is rooted in the ethics of Islam, ethics that reflect connectedness, responsibility, awareness, intellect, faith, love, generosity, wisdom and clarity. I pray that I am blessed with inspiration in speaking, seeing, hearing and acting that is grounded in knowledge and love.

For my community. I hope that we as diverse communities of Muslims learn from our rich, extraordinary history and role models of the past, that we nurture knowledge, learning and critical inquiry within ourselves and in the generations to come; that we truly expand and connect not only within our communities but with all of humanity in its struggles against oppression and injustice, and finally that the spark of social responsibility, service, gratitude and love inspires our communities.

Salwa

For myself. I hope and pray that I will express my faith and commitment to Allah (swt) by fulfilling all my Islamic duties and the will of God. I pray that I evoke the love of God in every aspect of my life. I pray that I will be blessed in raising a family inshallah, so that I may instill the values, traditions, and practices of our magnificent and impressive religion.

For my community. I pray that our community elevates our collective social consciousness to issues that affect all of humankind, and we govern our human interactions based on the Islamic spirit of love, tolerance, compassion and understanding. I pray that the community works together in brotherhood and sisterhood to uplift the moral and ethical conduct of our society and reaches out to those communities in which we live to exemplify the true essence and will of Islam.

It is in the ending that the doors open for a new beginning.

Majlis al-Âkhir

The Last

Proclaim! (or read!) in the name of thy Lord and Cherisher, Who created-Created man, out of a (mere) clot of congealed blood:
Proclaim! And thy Lord is Most Bountiful, He Who taught (the use of) the pen, Taught man that which he knew not.

(96:1-5)

I believe that this is the beginning of connections which should continue to be fostered. I invite you all to start telling your own stories, to provide narratives that challenge Eurocentric/American-centric perspectives and give voice to untold histories.

Public dialogue and debate must have forums and minoritized communities should be parts of them. We must challenge thinking that perpetuates and supports stereotypes, the status quo and the interests of dominant groups. Civil society must be given an opportunity to flourish with consciousness and critical dialogue. This book provides a model for bringing together diverse people and for creating spaces for conversation and debate.

Through making the lives and stories of Muslims visible, we hope we have given non-Muslim readers new insight and diverse perspectives on Islam and Muslim women.

As Muslims we have a responsibility to one another and to humanity to continue to live within the ethics of our faith, which guide our words and actions to serve our communities. The notion of being socially conscious and responsible can lead us to create balanced, healthy and intellectually, spiritually and materially prosperous communities.

By connecting with one another we can build bridges across communities. The women in this book pray that the connections we have begun to make can be steps towards creating positive relationships amongst Muslims and between Muslim communities and non-Muslim communities.

We encourage you to continue this dialogue. Send us your thoughts and questions, tell us what you support or disagree with, share with us your ideas. We hope that processes used in this project can be duplicated and used in future projects and forums. If you would like to learn more about this project or how to go about organizing something like this in your community, school, organization or among a circle of friends, we would love to share our experiences with you.

Finally, we want to leave you with prayers for knowledge, balance, harmony, equity, peace and love for all. Ameen!

The Muslim Women's Collective
Director: Salima Bhimani
email: muswomcollective@canada.com

The Last

References

Barndt, Deborah. "Naming, Making and Connecting: Pedagogical Possibilities of Photo-story Production." In Pat Campbell and Barbara Burnaby, *Participatory Processes in Adult Education*. Mahwah, NJ: Lawrence Erlbuam Associates, 2001.

Chaudhury, Shakil. *The Brown Book: Voices of Pakistani and Muslim Activists from Toronto and Lahore*. Newschool, 2000.

Herman S. Edward, Chomsky, Noam. *Manufacturing Consent. The Political Economy of the Mass Media* Random House, Toronto 2002.

Hall, Stuart. *Representation: Cultural Representation and Signifying Practice.* Thousand Oaks, Cal: Sage Publications, 1997.

Jensen, Derrick. *The Culture of Make Believe.* Context Books, New York 2002.

Mernissi, Fatima. *Women and Islam: A Historical and Theological Inquiry.* Oxford: Basil Blackwell, 1991.

Mohja, Kahf. *Western Representation of The Muslim Women: From Termagant To Odalisque*. Austin: University of Texas Press, 1999.

Sardar, Ziauddin, Davies W. Merryl. *Why Do People Hate America? Icon Books Ltd. Cambridge, 2002*

Tohidi, Nayrereh. "The Issues At Hand." In *Women in Muslim Societies: Diversity Within Unity.* Ed Bodman and Tohidi. Lynne Rienner Pub. London, 1998. pp‾277‾292

Great Books

Islam and Islamic History

A History of Islamic Societies. Ira Lapidus.
Rethinking Islam: Common Questions, Uncommon Answers. Mohammed Arkoun.
Islam: A Very Short History. Malise Ruthven.
A Short History of the Ismailis. Farhad Daftary.
Intellectual Traditions in Islam. Edited by Farhad Daftary.
Shimmering Light: An Anthology of Ismaili Poetry. Faquir M. Hunzai.
The Bounty of Allah: Daily Reflections from the Qu'ran and Islamic Tradition.
Aneela Khalid Arshed.

Muslim Women and Islam

Women and Gender in Islam. Leila Ahmed.
The Life and Work Of Rabi'a and Other Women Mystics in Islam. Margaret Smith.
My Soul Is a Woman: The Feminine in Islam. Annemarie Schimmel.
Qu'ran and Woman: Rereading the Sacred Text from a Woman's Perspective. Amina Wadud.
Feminism and Islamic Fundamentalism: The Limits of Postmodern Analysis. Haideh Moghissi.
Women in Muslim Societies: Diversity Within Unity. Edited by Herbert L.Bodman and Nayereh
Tohidi.

Media, Politics, Cultural Studies

The Brown Book. Shakil Choudhury.
*Covering Islam: How The Media and the Experts Determine How We See the Rest of the
World.* Edward Said.
Jihad vs McWorld. Benjamin Barber.
Islamic Peril. Karim H. Karim.
The Fifty Years War: Israel and the Arabs. Based on the BBC TV Series. Ahron Bregman and
Jihan El-Tahiri.
The Islamic Threat. Myth or Reality? John Esposito.
The Clash of Fundamentalisms: Crusades. Jihad, and Modernity. Tariq Ali.
The Edward Said Reader. Edited by Moustafa Boyoumi and Andrew Rubin.
Veils and Daggers: A Century of National Geographic's Representation of the Arab World.
Stupid White Men. Michael Moore.
The Culture of Make Believe. Derrick Jensen.

September-11 Related

Why Do People Hate America? Ziauddin Sardar and Merryl Wyn Davies
9-11. Noam Chomsky.

The Last

Network and Alliances

Council on American-Islamic Relations Canada http://www.caircan.ca/
Afghan Youth Organization http://www.geocities.com/afghanm/
Canadian Muslim Civil Liberties Association http://www.cmcla.org/
Council of Agencies Serving South Asians http://www.cassa.on.ca/mainpageW.html
Canadian Islamic Congress http://www.canadianislamiccongress.com/
The Canadian Arab Federation http://www.caf.ca/caf.htm
The Institute of Ismaili Studies http://www.iis.ac.uk
The Aga Khan Development Network http://www.akdn.org
Muslim Women's Help Network http://home.earthlink.net/~hanan/mwhelpnet.htm
South Asian Women's Network http://www.umiacs.umd.edu/users/sawweb/sawnet/
Canadian Council of Muslim Women http://www3.sympatico.ca/ccmw.london/
The World Council of Muslim Women http://www.connect.ab.ca/-lfahlman/wcomwf.htm
World Interfaith Association http://www.connect.ab.ca/-lfahlman/wifea.htm
Muslim Women's League http://www.mwlusa.org
Women for Women http://www.womenforwomen.org
Muslim Women Lawyers for Human Rights http://www.karamah. org
International Muslimah Artist Network (IMAN) http://www.hammoude.com
The Silk Road Project http://www.silkroadproject.org/music/instruments.html
Federation of Muslim Women http://www.fmw.org

Acknowledgements

There are many people who have provided their time, support, love, direction and spirit to me throughout this project. My deep gratitude goes to Allah for having faith in me to do this important work. Without the women who opened their lives, minds and souls in telling their stories this project would not be.

I would like give a special thanks to Shafik Kamani who has co-designed the book and done the layout for the book. Without his hard work and dedication, this book would not be what it is today.
To Mohamed Alibhai without whose support, guidance and assistance this book would not be where it is today.
To TSAR Publications for their support and commitment.
To Deborah Bardnt, my supervisor, support system and role model.
To Badur Ramji for assisting with the first draft of the book layout
To others who have supported me and this project in various ways:
My parents~Mehmud ~ Shahid ~ Roxy ~ Tim ~ Shakil ~Amir ~ and all other family and friends.

May your kindness, love, generosity, friendship and support find its way back to you a thousandfold.

Credits for photographs and text excerpts used in this book:

All of the Qur'anic verses have been extracted from the Abdullah Yusuf Ali Translation.

Majlis al-Khabir
Salwa Stetieh: Salwa's photo and her symbol.
Amber Nasrulla: Amber Nasrulla's photo.
Mezghan Hakimy: Mezghan Hakimy's photo.
Farah Murji: Farah Murji's photo.
Nazneen Khan: Nazneen Khan's photo.
Zaynab: Zaynab's photo.

Majlis al-Bari
Image from Magazine, Bijan Ad:Media Watch Youth
http://www.mediawatchyouth.ca/images.php?cat=rr

Majlis al-Mujib
Images from Magazines
Woman Smoking Pipe: Egypt's *Insight Magazine* Sept 2000

Majlis al-Adl
Salwa: Image of little girl
Mezghan: photo with Mezghan and students

Majlis al-Basit
Nazneen: Nazneen and Aunty
Amber: Qaisra Nasrulla
Farah: Tasleem Murji
Munira: Fatima Takache
Salwa: Helweh Juma
Mezghan: Mrs Hakimy

"Allah is the Light of the heavens and the earth. The example of His Light is a niche in which is a lamp. The lamp is in a glass. The glass is as it were a shining star. (This lamp is) lit from a blessed tree, an olive neither of the East nor of the West, whose oil would almost glow forth (of itself) though no fire touched it. Light upon Light. Allah Guides to His Light whom He will."

(The Holy Quran, 24:35)